Take Back Your Kids

**Confident Parenting in
Turbulent Times**

Take Back Your Kids

WILLIAM J. DOHERTY Ph.D.

SORIN BOOKS   Notre Dame, Indiana

International Standard Book Number: 1-893732-07-X
Library of Congress Catalog Number: 99-67496
Printed and bound in the United States of America.

For Eric and Elizabeth

CONTENTS

INTRODUCTION

I wrote this book because I see a growing confidence gap among American parents. We may now have the most child-sensitive generation of parents the world has ever known—and the most confused and insecure. This generation has determined to not repeat the mistakes of its own parents who expected unquestioning obedience. But in rejecting outmoded models of authority, parents are now skittish about exercising any authority at all. They are afraid that they cannot be both sensitive and in charge. The result is bad news for both kids and parents.

Children raised with insecure parents try to build a personal world where parents are less important. They grow up too soon, become preoccupied with consumer goods and peer acceptance, and focus their lives on frenetic activity outside the home. They know that their parents love them deeply and want to communicate sensitively with them, but they also know that their parents are unsure about what to require of them and how to say "no" to them. These children become the center of their own insecure universe.

An example: a family now in therapy has a ten-year-old boy, who is an angel in school, but who has started to call his mother a "bitch" at home. He didn't start out with the "b" word, but got to it over several years of increasingly unchecked disrespectful behavior when he was angry. Rather than exercising legitimate authority, his mother now responds by feeling sorry that her son is so distraught. She used to get angry, but now sees her own anger as a poor response to a troubled child. The father is simply befuddled by all of this.

Another example: my local newspaper has been running a series on alcohol and teens. Kids in earlier generations drank alcohol, often to excess. The difference now, as documented in the newspaper articles, is that parents supply the keg of beer, the house or hotel room, and the funds to enjoy a Mexican frolic of booze and sex during spring break. Most parents who were interviewed were reluctant to let their children go on a Mexican spring break this year, but were unable to say "no," particularly when their teenager had raised enough money to go and when most of the other kids announced they were going. Here is a quote from one mother who could not say "no": "It's all kids talk about for months beforehand and months after. You don't want her to be the only kid at lunch not going. How sad would that be?" This kind of insecure, confused parenting that can't say "no" ends up handing over a child to the peer culture.

One nervous parent told a reporter something very revealing about the confidence gap among contemporary parents: "When you're in a grocery store and see a kid screaming for gum, you say, 'My kid's not going to do it.' Your kid gets to that age, and you give them gum to shut them up. It's the same with this. As the years go by and the kids get older, you see that this is what they do." The lesson: You don't get to this point without years of surrendering your obligation to say "no" to your kid's demands.

Some of the teens interviewed on spring break sounded more like adults than their parents did. A high school senior, watching the bumping and grinding on the dance floor, said, "It's like one big orgy. I'd never let my daughter come." A college student whose parents had not let her go to Cancun during high school is now glad her parents insisted on a different kind of spring break. Her trip would have centered only around drinking, she said. "I cried for a day, but I got over it. I never would have been able to handle this. . . ."

The lesson: You sometimes have to withstand your kids' anger and tears in order to deserve gratitude at a later age.

I am convinced that we can close this terrible confidence gap without returning to authoritarian parenting. I believe that we can be thoroughly modern parents who value each child's sensitivities and developmental needs while still having high expectations for children as persons who have responsibilities to family and community.

I believe it is possible to balance the needs of the whole family—for example, for family ritual time—and the needs of children to pursue their personal goals. To do so we need to understand that today's child-rearing problems are bigger than any individual family, that they are community problems as well, and that solutions must also come from the community level. We need to fight against the parental peer pressure that is driving us as parents to continually provide more goods and better services for our children.

There is a middle way between being dictatorial and insensitive on the one hand, and cajoling and debating with children on the other hand. We can control our child's behavior, such as attending church, doing homework, or visiting grandmother, without trying to control our child's attitudes, feelings, and beliefs, such as the child's level of enthusiasm for church, homework, or grandmother. We need to distinguish between our role as confident authority figure (around legitimate behavioral expectations) and our role as model and consultant (around the child's inner world of beliefs, feelings, and values).

These are convictions that have been nurtured by my experience as a family therapist and teacher for nearly twenty-five years. But more than in my professional training as a family therapist, and more than in my academic training as a family social scientist, it is in the everyday crucible of parenting Eric and Elizabeth, my now-grown children, that I have learned what I am sharing with you in this book. Not just in my one-to-one parenting, but also in co-parenting with Leah, my wife and life partner. Every idea in this book was passed by these three main teachers in my life. I also want to acknowledge my first teachers, my parents, who left me a model of confident parenting that I could build on when I grew to be a father myself in a different era with new challenges.

Several other people made important contributions to this book. My editor, John Kirvan, first approached me about doing a book on values and parenting, and gave me sage advice about writing the book. Jim Levine, my agent and trusted adviser, saw the possibilities and gave me valuable feedback. Ann O'Grady-Schneider was most generous in reading and commenting on the second draft. And many friends, acquaintances, and clients have shared with me the stories you will find in this book. I have changed identifying details in stories to protect their confidentiality.

I would love to hear what you think about this book, and I would love to hear your stories about how you maintain your authority and your sensitivity as a parent in a culture that says you can't have both.

You can e-mail me at: **bdoherty@che1.che.umn.edu**, or you can write to me at Family Social Science Department, University of Minnesota, 290 McNeal Hall, St. Paul, MN 55108.

Why It's Harder Being a Parent Today

We are facing an epidemic of insecure parenting. Many parents are afraid not just *for* their children, but *of* their children. A sixty-three-year-old man I know hadn't talked to his son Michael in several weeks, so he called him long distance to chat. Barely three minutes into the call, his three-year-old grandson, Jeff, starts to make a fuss in the background. Michael suddenly announces that he will have to get off the phone because Jeff hates it when his parents are on the phone and not paying enough attention to him. Michael makes a quick goodbye and hangs up. His father is dumbstruck but says nothing, out of fear of sounding critical of his son's parenting.

My wife and I had a similar experience when visiting old friends. We had not seen them since the birth of their daughter, Tanya, five years before. Tanya seemed like a normal, shy little girl when we arrived, saying hello and then quickly toddling off to play by herself. The four adults sat down to catch up with our lives. No more than five minutes had elapsed when Tanya burst into the room and angrily confronted her parents. She said that there was too much "adult talk" going on and that it was not fun for her. Her parents jolted to attention as if responding to a commanding officer. They apologized for being insensitive and promised to cease the adult talk so that Tanya could join the conversation. However, Tanya did not want to join the rest of us in any kind of conversation. Instead she wanted to play alone with her mother, who proceeded to excuse herself for the next thirty minutes, until Tanya released her to begin cooking dinner.

My own children, ages eleven and thirteen at the time, watched this scene with quiet amazement. I don't think they had ever encountered this combination of an autocratic child and timid parents. It was like they were watching a new force of nature. You see, although my wife and I have made our share of mistakes as parents, we never caught the virus of fearfulness and insecurity that has infected many good contemporary parents.

Here's one more story, this one about the fear of disappointing our children's consumer desires. A mother was frantically searching for the Pokemon video game (the latest rage among preteen boys) in a major retail store. After the clerk told the mother that the game was sold out, the mother begged the clerk to write her son a letter, on store stationary, testifying that the game was out of stock. "He will never believe me," explained the mother. The clerk politely declined, leaving the mother to fend for herself against the suspicion and fury of a nine-year-old scorned.

What do you think is going on in the three stories I have described? Have you seen similar things or had similar experiences? If these stories were set forty or more years ago, you might assume that these were unusual families with very unskilled parents. But these three families are actually fairly typical for the current generation, with parents who are devoted, caring, and sensitive—and afraid of displeasing their children. They are parents who set too few limits, because they are afraid to upset their children too much.

My, how things have changed—both for better and worse. In the course of one generation of parents, we have gotten a lot better at being sensitive to our children and their needs and a lot worse at setting limits for them.

We no longer want our children to grow up in fear of our anger, but we now live in fear of theirs.

We know when to explain ourselves and negotiate with our children, but not when to cut off further discussion.

We know the importance of open expression, but don't know when to insist that a child be quiet or stop interrupting adult conversation.

We support our children's right to express their ire and frustration, but don't know when they cross the line into disrespect.

We are expert at finding community activities for our children to participate in, but don't know when to say "enough."

We are willing to bend our family time to fit our children's schedules, but are hesitant to limit their schedules for the sake of the family.

We are better at knowing what to buy for our children than what to deny them.

We are better at helping our children make their own decisions, but are confused about when we should make decisions for them.

When dealing with schools, we are better at advocating for our children, but fail to side with the school when our child's behavior is out of line.

We are more involved with our children's sports activities, but we have lost the balance between home life and kids' outside activities.

We know more about raising our children than about nurturing our marriages, which sometimes must be protected from our children's demands.

We earnestly desire to meet our children's needs, but often can't separate their needs from their desires.

The Consumer Culture of Childhood

In the new culture of childhood, children are viewed as *consumers* of parental services, and parents are viewed as *providers* of parental services and *brokers* of community services for children. What gets lost is the other side of the human equation: children bearing responsibilities to their families and communities. In a balanced world, children are expected not only to receive from adults but also to actively contribute to the world around them, to help care for the younger and the infirm, to add their own marks to the quality of family life, and to contribute to the common good in their school and communities. If children live only as consumers of parental and community services, then they are not active citizens of families and communities.

If we see ourselves only as providers of services to our children (and indeed, this is one important part of parenting), we end up confused about our authority, anxious about displeasing our children, insecure about whether we are providing enough opportunities, and worried that we are not keeping up with the output of other parents. In a market economy, the service provider must offer what is newest and best, and at all costs, must avoid disappointing the customer. When applied to the family, this is a recipe for insecure parents and entitled kids.

Most parents are willing to displease their child in situations that are clearly harmful to the child's well-being— nobody lets a toddler walk out into traffic. The rub comes when something we are requiring is not obviously related to the child's immediate well being. Examples include doing chores, showing up for dinner, joining the family on vacation, and having a set bed time that is enforced even if the child is not tired. It is hard for many parents to require these activities when their children resist.

Not only are parents increasingly confused about what they can expect of their children, children themselves are absorbing the consumer attitude of individual self-interest. Here are some lines that parents have reported to me recently:

- A seventeen-year-old says to his parents, "Why should I mow the lawn? It's not *my* lawn."

- After opening a Hanukkah gift from his father, an eleven-year-old boy fails to say thank you. When challenged about this by the father, the boy responds, "But I don't like it."

- A teenager refuses to eat dinners with the family because she is "not hungry" and "I'd rather be on the phone with my friends."

Kids get these attitudes from the same culture that feeds self-centeredness among adults. I worry that parents who resent being servants to their children will start to compete with them for who gets their needs met first. A recent car commercial on television was directed at fathers: "Your kids always get what they want—why not you?" In another commercial for a food company, a mother, after admitting that her teens' schedules do not permit family meals, offers her philosophy of parenting as follows: "I just want them to enjoy themselves, and I want to be part of it." This is the model of the parent as a buddy who wants to share in the good times. How can she turn around and set limits or expect her teenagers to be of service to someone other than themselves?

When parents serve their children too much, they identify too closely with their successes and failures. It becomes hard to tell whether the child's athletic events are more for the child or the parents. Lower academic grades produce parental outrage against the teacher. Parents cannot deny a request for the latest designer clothing item, because having one's teenager be "out of it" with peers is as unacceptable to the parent as it is to the young person. In serving too much and expecting too little, we end up confusing our children's needs with our own. Their insecurities become ours, and our insecurities become theirs.

There are other casualties of the culture that turns children into consumers and parents into providers and playmates. Children become frantically overscheduled as we try to maximize their opportunities. Family time and family rituals deteriorate. Parents can't say no to a new enrichment activity such as karate or traveling soccer on the grounds that it interferes with family dinners. In fact, the older children get, the more everyone expects that family time will vanish. But even for young children, the activity options are breathtaking: In the small college town of Northfield, Minnesota, a mother counted fourteen community activities for three-year-olds. In a Minneapolis suburb, a six-year-old girl was delighted to receive her first daily planner, which she no doubt needs because she is in seven car pools per week!

This is not just a middle class problem. Working class and even poor parents tell me that they feel overwhelmed by their children's schedules. Can you guess the group that studies find spends the most hours per week in an automobile? Single mothers. Middle class parents from two-parent families may be able to afford more options for their children, but the famine of family time cuts across the whole population of families with children.

It isn't just parents who create this situation, it's also the other "providers" in the community, such as coaches in recreation programs. In one community, the basketball coach insisted on holding practices on Thanksgiving afternoon and the day after Christmas, threatening any boy who missed with lost playing time. The parents did not protest, I am told, because they did not want to jeopardize their boys' opportunity to play on a successful team. A soccer coach for a traveling soccer team told the parents at the first orientation that their families can take vacation only during the second and third weeks in August. No one protested. What if your out-of-state family reunion is in July every year? What if the cabin you share with other families is available only in June? What if your other child's coach says you cannot be gone during the second and third weeks in August? We have become like sheep led by the people who schedule our children's lives.

Not that coaches intentionally undermine family life. They are just doing their job of developing young people's athletic potential, building team cohesion, and winning ball games. And they are doing this in an atmosphere where a vocal minority of parents push the coaches to require the utmost from the children and families, and where a solid majority of adults and children assume that family life should revolve around the personal activities of children. In the consumer culture of childhood, coaches and other activity leaders become specialized service providers in top priority areas. Parents, as brokers of these specialized services, are expected to do whatever is necessary for their children to participate in as many opportunities as possible.

When balanced with other life domains, team sports can help build citizenship among children and a sense of community among families. When this balance is out of whack, commitment to youth sports trumps all other commitments. I know a mother who took her daughter, Emily, out of two soccer games one summer because of an out-of-state family wedding. The mother faced intense opposition from Emily, serious questions from the coach (these were big games, you see), and disappointed comments from the other parents (her daughter was a key player). It took several hours on the road for Emily to speak in a civil manner to her mother, but the eventual outcome was gratifying. The rest of the extended family gushed over Emily for coming to the wedding, knowing that she had given up important games. On the trip home, she asked her mother why one of her cousins had not attended. After her mother replied that this cousin just did his own thing without regard for the rest of the family, Emily proudly proclaimed, "Well, there are times when you just have to be there for your family." What a powerful reinforcement of her mother's courage against serious opposition. But it should not take heroic courage to take your teenager out of a ballgame for the sake of a family wedding.

Isn't it curious how showing up at every game has become a litmus test for being a good parent? I wonder when this happened. When I was growing up, my friends and I never expected our parents to attend our team games. If they came once in a while, we felt honored. Nowadays, we have television commercials depicting a guilt-ridden father who, because he flies the right airline, manages to make his son's soccer game just in time to see him score a goal. Before dad arrives, the boy keeps looking anxiously towards the sideline, obviously not able to keep his mind on the game because his father is letting him down.

In May, 1999, in the wake of the mass murders in a high school in Littleton, Colorado, the media's initial reports about the family life of one of the teen killers emphasized that the parents were "involved" in their son's life, as indicated by the fact that they attended all his sporting events, and sometimes even practices. This clear evidence of good parenting was puzzling to media commentators who also reported that these same parents did not stop their son from having weapons and bomb making material in his bedroom. It was not puzzling to me. Although I have no knowledge of this particular family, I can readily understand how parents can be athletic boosters to their son and be afraid to confront him about his antisocial behavior. I can even understand never looking in his room because he angrily insists on his privacy. Being part of his sporting life is safe. He doesn't get mad at you when you follow his lead, only when you want him to follow yours.

Actually I believe the parental sports attendance law got promulgated some time in the 1970s or 1980s. When I grew up in the 1950s and early 1960s, parents were too busy working and raising other kids to regularly attend games. And we did not feel deprived. Let me be clear: there is nothing wrong with attending your child's activities. My wife and I attended our children's sporting events, supported our kids and enjoyed the camaraderie with other parents on the sidelines. But those were the days when the season consisted of one game per week for a few months, and when our kids' coaches wanted everyone to have a good time. And we certainly did not miss major family events because of a soccer game or baseball game. My concern is for what experiences families now miss out on because of the singular importance of attending every sporting event for every child.

Sometimes children themselves come to resent the pressure of our exaggerated emphasis on sports. The thirteen-year-old daughter of a colleague chose a confirmation retreat at her church over a traveling soccer weekend. The coach wrote her a tirade about commitment. You see, we are beginning to define "responsibility" and "commitment" in terms of team sports, as if the child has no obligations in other zones of life. The father of the thirteen-year-old called the coach to talk about the importance of balance in kids' lives. The coach cut him off with the words "I don't believe in balance." Hurt and sad about the coach's attitude, the girl resigned from the traveling soccer team.

But it's not just the fault of coaches, the clergy, the schools, or even the parents. It's all of us; it's a cultural problem. The advertising media pummel all of us with messages of individual gratification. Huge amounts of money are spent in advertising just for preschool children. Parents' work schedules are often not family friendly, leaving parents feeling guilty and substituting indulgence for time. Two-earner families try to squeeze too many activities into their schedules. Homemakers feel they have no excuse but to be full-time social organizers and chauffeurs for their children and their children's friends. Single parents often feel too overwhelmed to fight for family time. Non-custodial parents fall into the pattern of entertaining their children every other weekend. And parents in all kinds of families worry that their children will fall behind their peers, and feel guilty about not providing the same opportunities that other parents are providing for their children. This worry and guilt lead to paralysis when our children let us know that they are not happy consumers of our services.

The problem seems to be worsening. Just as there are rising consumer expectations for more and better products and services, there are rising expectations for meeting individual needs in families. According to the parents I talk to, children nowadays are less inclined to compromise their wants for the sake of the group. One mother calls herself "Kathy's Country Kitchen" because the children all demand their own special food items for dinner. Children have always protested that they don't like certain foods, but now parents tell me that, even when children actually like a certain food, they will protest because they wanted something else tonight, thank you. Call it "The Fast Food Family." At these restaurants, children get precisely what they want, so why not at home?

Marketing directly to children is a powerful way businesses contribute to the consumer culture of childhood in the family. Young children in particular have few defenses against the creative minds of advertisers whose job it is to cultivate little consumers to influence their parents' buying decisions. A colleague told me of an advertising convention in which the keynoter spoke to the audience on the topic of how to "reduce the influence of parents" on their children's consuming habits. It's no wonder that any insecurity on the part of parents means that the consumer culture of childhood will take over the family.

The Therapeutic Culture of Parenting

The culprit is more than just the consumer culture of childhood. We also live in the era of therapeutic parenting. The parent becomes a junior therapist, and the child is seen as requiring special treatment that only a professional—or a trained parent—can provide. Starting back in the 1970s with *Parent Effectiveness Training: The Tested New Way to Raise Responsible Children* (a popular book by Thomas Gordon), and continuing through subsequent books and programs, parents have been taught to act like therapists with their kids.

A therapist is supposed to be consistently attentive, low key, accepting, non-directive, and non-judgmental. When the child acts up in a therapy session, say, by speaking disrespectfully to the therapist, the therapist's job is to explore the underlying reasons rather than focus on the child's immediate behavior. For good reasons, therapists assume that the therapist-patient relationship at the beginning is fragile, and they rarely risk showing direct, personal anger towards the child.

However the therapeutic model becomes distorted when applied outside of the therapy context. I remember a scene at a large facility for emotionally disturbed children and adolescents. A group of preteen boys had climbed on the hood of a car containing several child psychotherapists. The driver got out of her car and gently asked the boys to get off her vehicle so she could proceed on her trip. When they did not move, she looked flustered but stayed with her therapeutic demeanor, saying "I don't know what this is about, but I need you to get off my car now." By now, the kids were really enjoying themselves. Then along came a child care staff member, someone who lived with the children and thus had to manage their unruly behavior. She barked, "Get off that car this instant!" The boys were gone in a flash. After that, I've never forgotten that the therapeutic stance belongs in just one place—a therapy session.

In addition to distorting parents' reactions to their children's misconduct, the therapeutic culture of parenting suggests that children's psyches are fragile, easily broken by a parent who says the wrong thing. The reality, according to loads of research, is that, if underlying parental care and attachment are present, most children are resilient in the face of ordinary mistakes in parenting. If our children know we love them and are committed to them forever, they can handle our unjustified but non-abusive anger, our inevitable episodes of self-centeredness, and our inattentiveness.

If children can handle most of our mistakes, they can certainly handle our strong responses to them when these responses are fully called for. Children mostly know when they are off base, and feel safer when their parents step in assertively. The boys climbing on the therapist's car got into a lot more trouble because she could not directly assert her indignation. Their actions became a major incident on the campus, with serious consequences for the children involved. If she had acted like a parental authority figure right away, they would have gotten off the car and the incident would have been forgotten.

I want to be clear that I think child psychology and family studies have much to offer parents. In fact, what I am advocating in child rearing is consistent with the best research: children need both love and limits, they need confident rather than insecure parents, and they do best when contributing to the common good rather than just focusing on themselves. What I object to are unrealistic and undermining myths in popular parenting advice.

The first myth of therapeutic parenting is that children are fragile. This false assumption contributes to the "timid parent syndrome" I have been discussing. If I raise my voice or exert my power, my child will be traumatized or will turn against me. This flies in the face of what we know about the resilience of nearly all children when being disciplined by an involved, loving parent.

The second myth is that parents should promote the authentic expression of the child's individuality by de-emphasizing social conformity. The myth is that each child is a unique flower ready to bloom if we create the right conditions and don't interfere too much. It is wrong to force children to do what they don't authentically want to do, or to deny them something they really, really want, unless there is a clearly compelling reason. It is counterproductive to insist that children communicate in certain conforming ways, such as insisting that your adolescent daughter stop cursing at you when she is angry. It's more important to get to the root of her anger than to begin with telling her she cannot curse you. The cursing is just the symptom, you see, and you've got to get to the underlying causes. If you focus too much on the overt behavior in an angry way, you will damage your child.

Do you see the difference here between the therapy setting and the family setting? If an adolescent client responds with a curse word to my first question as a family therapist, I am likely not to react but to explore where that came from. If one of my kids curses me, they will hear from me immediately about that behavior, which will cease forthwith, before we get into whatever is going on underneath. But if I am influenced by the culture of therapeutic parenting, then I will hold back, be impotent, and confuse my child.

The third myth of therapeutic parenting specifically involves teenagers. This myth is that parents do not have much direct influence over their teenagers' behavior. That is, teenagers will mostly do what they want anyway. They should be given room to make their own choices, even if the parents would make different ones. Otherwise, their development will be stifled. This myth comes into full play in the later years of high school, by which point many parents have completed the process of resigning as parents and become full-fledged buddies to their children. Thus, half the high-school seniors in town I know of spend their spring break, un-chaperoned and with parents' permission, at Mexican frolics that put them at risk for acting out sexually and drinking and abusing drugs. Some of these parents also reserve hotel rooms for their teenagers after the prom, knowing that sexual activity is thereby more likely to occur. A handful of parents even buy the kegs of beer for their teenagers' parties, putting everyone's children at risk. When questioned, these parents fall back on the myth that teenagers have to "test their wings," that "kids will do what kids will do." They claim that parents who oppose this normal growing up process alienate their teenagers, and that it's better to go along and try to have a good relationship because "there is not much you can do anyway." What parents who embrace this myth do not say is that they are afraid to set limits on their teenager because they can't stand the heat of the negative reactions that would follow. Having surrendered their parental authority one cave-in at a time since the child was a toddler, they are now afraid to say no. As one mother put it, "You let them do start doing one thing after another, and pretty soon—poof!—they're going to Cancun."

What we know from research and common sense observation is that parents have a strong influence on their teenagers' behavior. For example, teenagers whose parents talk to them regularly about avoiding drugs are, in fact, much less likely to use drugs. Teenagers whose parents give them both nurturing and firm limits are less likely to be involved in sexual activity. They are more likely to study hard. The list could go on. Of course teenagers need more freedom than eight-year-olds, but they also need active involvement and monitoring from parents who believe they can make a difference in their children's lives. A client whose daughter had taken the SAT exam stoned on marijuana said to me, "She made a bad choice, but she has to learn to make her own decisions." I confronted her statement and belief in that myth, and together we worked to turn that talented girl—and her parents—around.

Successful Parenting in Today's Environment

We've diagnosed the problem of insecure, over-indulgent parenting as stemming from the consumer culture of childhood and the therapeutic culture of parenting. How do parents in this environment judge the success of their efforts to raise their children well? In the past, when social conformity was a higher value than individuality, parents could feel successful when they saw their children progress through the established roles of life: school, job, marriage, and parenting.

In the contemporary culture that combines consumer and therapeutic influences, success is harder to judge. How do I sense that I am doing an adequate job as a parental service provider, as an encourager of my child's unique personality and high self-esteem? Unfortunately, the answer often comes down to whether I have provided enough "opportunities" to my child—academic, social, athletic—and whether my child is outspoken and individualistic.

Especially in the consumer culture, successful parenting must be public and observable, because parents compete with one another as service providers. How else to interpret parents' boasting about how many Beanie Babies their child owns, or their child's precocious soccer prowess, popularity with the opposite sex, and likely entry into Harvard? How else to interpret some parents' strange mixture of concern and pride when describing their teenage daughter's new purple hairdo and their son's run in with the police for drinking in the car after the basketball game? Both the hairdo and the public drinking suggest that my child is an "original," his or her "own person," and certainly not a parent-pleasing conformist. The irony, of course, is that some experts end up supporting a kind of negative conformity in their children, not a true individuality.

What does the "good parent" look like in today's environment? It's the parent who does nearly everything for the child, and expects little back except that the child take advantage of the goods and services provided—and maybe express gratitude for the same. It's a parent who is careful to avoid threatening a child's psyche by showing anger, and who supports fully the child's right to honest self-expression against over-sensitivity to the feelings of others.

In this cultural environment why should children not complain vigorously, even push the limits of respect, when their parents disappoint their wishes, especially when the parent is so reluctant to ask the child to adapt to other people's needs? An ambivalent, insecure parent is a pushover in today's environment. The consumer culture will teach your child to act like a demanding brat, and the therapeutic culture will keep you from being assertive enough to exercise your parenting responsibility.

Eventually, when a child or adolescent consistently behaves in an uncooperative or ungrateful way, the consumer orientation can lead even loving parents to start asking themselves what they are getting out of this parenting bargain. Unlike twenty-five years ago, I now hear parents of teenagers wonder out loud, "Why am I trying so hard if my kid will not work with me?" and "How long do I have to keep giving until I get something back?" Thus the worm turns: parents may come to resent their children for being self-centered and ungrateful, even though we parents made them that way, and then withdraw from our children. The parental provider role is so unsatisfying over the long haul that some parents resign from being a parent at all.

I don't want to be an alarmist, but a sense of alarm is hard to avoid. Loving, concerned parents have lost their balance. There is reason to worry about the adults our children will become. We must learn something very difficult: how to create a seamless web connecting children's special needs as individuals with their responsibilities as citizens of families and communities. Come to think of it, isn't this the major challenge we are all facing in this time in history when we are liberating individuals but losing our sense of connection?

BEING A CONFIDENT PARENT IN AN INSECURE WORLD

Ann is a successful woman of her time. Raised in a world when women had unprecedented opportunities, she received her law degree and soon was combining law and business in a very successful career. She married Paul, who was very supportive of her career and, when they had children, shared equally in the duties of parenting.

Confidence and decisiveness were the hallmarks of Ann's personality—at work. Parenting was another matter. With four-year-old Jason, Ann was often unsure of herself. She was inconsistent with the house rules. Although embarrassed to admit it, she felt intimidated by Jason's angry demands and stubborn refusal to cooperate. When Jason acted like a bright, cooperative child, Ann felt like a great mother, delighting in helping him learn about his world. But when he was irritable and uncooperative, Ann felt at a loss because he did not respond to her reasonable requests for him to change his behavior. To make things worse, she felt that Paul was even less consistent than she was with discipline. She ended up being the "mean" parent who was nevertheless ineffective and insecure whenever Jason was in one of his moods.

Earlier in my career, I would have seen Ann's parenting problems as stemming strictly from Ann and Paul's lack of effective parenting skills. But I would have missed the bigger cultural picture that has since become clear to me. Parents who came of age after the 1960s tend to have trouble with limit-setting and with clear expectations for children's behavior. They are better at giving than at requiring, better at listening than at ending debates, better at responding than at leading. In many ways they are wonderful, caring parents, but they accommodate too much and limit too little. They have caught the virus of insecure, ambivalent parenting.

In the discussion that follows, I invite you to assess your own degree of security or confidence as a parent, to figure out where your insecurity might come from, to listen for the cultural messages that undermine your confidence, and to learn how to be confident and secure while knowing that you don't have all the answers. Perhaps you already feel fine about yourself as a parent, with little insecurity. If so, our discussion might help you understand why some of your friends and relatives—or your spouse—do not feel as secure as you. If you are a grandparent, our discussion may help you better understand the parenting challenges the younger generation faces. Parental insecurity, the feeling of being pulled between love and limits, is nothing to be ashamed of. It is a common affliction among American parents born in the second half of the twentieth century.

Your Generation

We are all raised in a mainstream culture whose influence is mostly invisible to us. (This dominant culture is powerful even in ethnic groups that have their own special subcultures.) If you were born after 1945—a so-called baby boomer, a generation X'er or a gen Y'er—you grew up in a world very different from that of previous generations. I myself, born in 1945, came along at the beginning of the baby boom. If you reached middle childhood or adolescence after the mid-1960s, you probably absorbed some of the individualistic, "me" focus of the contemporary era, along with a good dose of skepticism about authority of all sorts—governmental, professional, and parental. You were taught that high self-esteem is the master key to a happy life, that personal creativity is good and social conformity is bad, and that public leaders who talk about values are probably hypocrites. You were taught that a parent's main job—after food, clothing, shelter, and love—is to help each child fulfill his or her unique potential, not to help the child "fit in."

Can you see how these cultural teachings, although capturing important elements of truth, can make it hard to deal with a demanding, self-oriented, and entitled four-year-old or fifteen-year-old (as nearly all children will be some of the time)? Baby boomer parents and those that followed live in fear of doing or saying the wrong thing. They are afraid of stifling their child's fragile self-worth, of imposing arbitrary adult authority on a child's individual initiative. They are afraid that their children will fall behind the peer group in academics, athletics, or any other area of competitive achievement. These tendencies among parents vary across our society, of course, and they are found most fully in middle class, educated families who often are the trend setters for the rest of society.

In addition to thinking about how mainstream American culture prepared you to be an insecure parent, consider your own parents. Reflect on your reactions to the way your parents raised you. Are you like Ann, born in 1958, who did not want to raise Jason in the same way her parents raised her? To Ann, her parents stood for the traditional values of obedience and conformity. They gave orders and were reluctant to negotiate. Although they loved their children and sacrificed for them, they were not particularly sensitive to each child's developmental needs. For example, they were slow to let Ann and her siblings have more freedom when they entered adolescence. Once Ann began to have her own opinions, her parents lectured to her rather than discussed with her. They hated her music, her hair, and some of her "hippie" friends.

After Ann entered the adult world of work and marriage, her parents relaxed quite a bit, and she now has a fairly good adult relationship with them. We are not talking about a troubled family here, just a family caught in a major generational shift of values. When she became a mother, Ann set out to be sensitive, not authoritarian; flexible, not rigid; compromising, not prescriptive. She was going to consider her child's feelings and needs before she spoke harshly. She would raise her voice sparingly, although she knew that limit setting was sometimes necessary.

Looking back as we worked together in family therapy, Ann realized that she had decided to act more like a grandparent than a parent. Grandparents traditionally emphasize only the positive parts of parenting—play, special treats, gifts, good times, and minimal rules and discipline. Current grandparents complain that they don't have the chance to "spoil" this new crop of grandchildren because the parents are already doing the spoiling! They are on guard and nervous when their grandchildren visit because these children are out of control—and the parents do not seem to notice.

To some extent, of course, every generation tries to improve on the previous one. Parents of the 1950s did on-demand infant feeding as opposed to the scheduled feedings of their own parents' generation. Fathers were trying to be emotionally closer to the children than their own fathers had been. As psychologist and author Mary Pipher has noted, every generation has a special way of showing love to the next generation; it's just that the next generation may have trouble valuing it. I invite you, then, to examine how the way you were raised has influenced your own parenting practices.

- In what ways are you trying to parent differently than your own parents; in doing so are you throwing out some of the good in order to move beyond the bad?

- In improving on your parents' sensitivity to children's special needs, have you become unsure about when to expect your children to conform and cooperate?

- In trying to do a better job of emphasizing your children's positive qualities, are you left wordless about their negative qualities?

- In trying to avoid unnecessary harshness, do you come across wishy-washy to your children?

- Are you afraid your everyday, non-abusive anger will wound your child?

- In giving your children more freedom than your parents gave you, are you indecisive about what freedoms to limit and reluctant to fight the good fight, if necessary, to maintain those limits?

Let's credit our parents' generation with being clear about what they expected of their children. My own parents were clear and unwavering in their values and expectations, a gift that I am grateful for and that has helped me to be a confident father. Our parents' journey, however, cannot be our journey, because the times are different. But if I had to choose whether to grow up with confident but less sensitive parents, versus sensitive but insecure, ambivalent parents, I'd choose the former in a flash. It's better to have something tangible to react against than to push against the fog. Parental insecurity is scary to children who do not have an anchor point to accept, protest, and eventually move past. When parents are afraid to parent, children are abandoned to the toxicity of the consumer culture and the peer culture.

Where You Are Now

Usually our insecurity as parents is rooted not just in the larger culture and in our personal reactions to our childhood, but also in our current situation. Here are some questions to help you assess your level of confidence versus insecurity as a parent:

Are you spending enough time with your children? If you do not have enough one-to-one time with your children so that they feel thoroughly bonded to you, they will give you untold grief that no amount of parental confidence will overcome. There is no formula for the amount of time to spend. It depends on the developmental level of the child and the circumstances of the family. Working mothers and fathers can certainly fulfill their children's needs for contact time. But if both parents are working sixty hours per week, or a single parent is working two jobs, or an at-home parent is more into personal schedule than children's needs, then there is a good chance these parents will experience so much resistance from the children that they will give up trying to exercise consistent limits. Children let us control them only when they sense our high level of nurturing involvement with them. Parental confidence must flow from the source waters of a solid, bonded relationship that requires considerable time and energy.

Do you feel guilty about the amount of time you spend with your children? If the guilt is grounded, as in the first point above, in a genuine lack of time with your children, then the first step is to change your schedule. Realistic guilt should lead to realistic changes. But sometimes parental guilt is based on unrealistic expectations and exaggerated ideas about children's needs for full time parental presence and undivided attention. In this case, be aware that your guilt can make it difficult to have high expectations for your children's behavior and to set limits on them. The mother who is guilty about working outside the home may find herself being "Nice Mom" instead of "Real Mom" when she is home from work. A father who travels a lot just wants peace when he is home. A non-custodial father who feels guilty about the divorce can't bring himself to be the "heavy" on his weekends with the children. Excessive parental guilt feeds parental insecurity.

How much are you afraid of being unpopular with your children? As we all know, good parenting demands stretches of unpopularity, which range from minutes during the toddler years to perhaps weeks and months during the adolescent years. Fear of falling off the popularity charts creates paralysis when we face a child's urgent, unreasonable demands. Of course, our children sense it when we cave in so as not to displease them. They are temporarily satisfied but underneath they are disappointed in us. And they feel more insecure themselves.

If you are co-parenting with a spouse, are you both together on your parenting values and practices? Even if you are otherwise a personally confident parent, you are likely to give in when confronted with a persistent, demanding child and a spouse who will not support you when the conflict with the child heats up. If your spouse is a pacifist who hates conflict, as in the case of Paul above, then you are cast in the "mean" role, which is difficult to sustain unless you are unusually confident and focused. And even then it takes a toll on you and your marriage. The better alternative, which I will discuss later, is to work with your spouse to be able to get both of you on the same page.

Do you know what to expect from your children as citizens of family and community, and what values underlie these expectations? If you don't know what you expect, it's hard to ask for it. And if your expectations are not grounded in core values, then it's hard to hold onto them when you face opposition. For example, what is your value for your family's participation in a religious community? Getting the children to go to worship services is apt to be an ongoing struggle as the children get older unless you are clear about what participation in religion means to you.

Outside Forces That Affect Confident Parenting

Even if you are clear about your values and fundamentally confident about your parenting practices, there are a host of outside forces that can undermine your values and subvert your confidence. These are the individuals and groups that lose sight of the child's responsibilities to family and community, and that encourage an excessive individualism and consumer orientation among children. Here are five of the main "outside forces" that attack secure and confident parenting:

1. The **advertising media** must rank high on any list of negative influences. The average American, according to *Consumer Reports*, is deluged with three thousand advertisement messages per day. A big part of the advertising dollar is directed at influencing children to pursue their consumer needs. Some psychologists have devoted their careers to helping industry shape the purchasing—and pleading—habits

of children as young as three years old. The result often is excessive purchases by and for children, who become over-stimulated by the largesse at birthdays and holidays. Perhaps the most common public conflict between parents and children is over the child's demand for a purchase and the parent's refusal, followed by a cycle of demand and refusal until sometimes the parent caves in—thereby teaching the child that all good things come to those who whine long enough. And when parents themselves get into the consumer frenzy for their children, we have the spectacle of Beanie Babies and other products that parents compete over.

2. **Television programming** is a primary teacher of American children, who spend on average twenty-three hours per week watching it. I will have lots more to say about television in later chapters, but for now let me pass on Mary Pipher's observation that we have the first generation in human history where the vast majority of stories told to children are passed on, not by people who love them and want to impart values, but by people who want to make customers of them.

3. **Other parents who are permissive** can also undermine confident parents. This becomes especially clear when children become teenagers. The permissiveness of some parents makes it hard for the parents who do try to parent in a confident way. For a typical teenager, this kind of permissive parent is worth bragging about, unlike the Neanderthal, uptight parent who insists on calling the other parents before a party or an overnight. As I said before, the most common justification for parental irresponsibility is that "the kids will do it anyway." These permissive parents make it difficult for average parents

to withstand the pressure from their children and the community to bend their standards and put their children at risk.

4. **Other parents competing over their children's activities and achievements** are also able to undermine. One father, who is trying to achieve balance between his children's activities and family time, described another father sauntering up to him at a soccer game, with this line of inquiry: "So what other sports is your son in? Oh really, not hockey? Doesn't he like hockey, or isn't he any good at it?" Parents whose egos are wrapped up in their children's individual exploits, and who do not protect their family time, make it more difficult for other parents to create a balanced life.

5. **Coaches, youth ministers, and other providers of children's activities** can also undermine confident parenting by insisting children participate in functions and events to the detriment of families and responsibilities. By insisting on their prerogatives over children's schedules, these providers move the center of control of family time away from parents. A "good" parent in this mentality is one who gets his or her kid to every practice, watches every game from the sidelines, and never questions the control the schedule has over their lives.

Activating Necessary Skills for Effective Parenting

I want to help you to become more clear about what you expect of yourself and your children, and to activate the skills necessary to be a confident, courageous parent. Ann and Paul, whose story you heard earlier, became clearer about their expectations for themselves and their children and more confident as parents as a result of their efforts in family therapy. They learned to apply to their parenting the life skills they used in other areas of life. They raised their expectations of Jason, and followed through more consistently. He resisted at first, but ended up a happier child. Ironically, by being clear and assertive with him and not letting him dominate the family, Ann and Paul were angry at Jason much less often. Out-of-control parents are usually meaner than in-control parents because they get more frustrated, more often. These parents then try to exercise arbitrary authority rather than reasoned authority, and when this does not work, they yell and scream or give up trying.

I also want to stress that it's often too hard to do this alone, this move from insecure parenting to confident parenting. Most of us need support from other like-minded parents in our communities, or, for the hardest problems, a therapist. That's why I urge you to start talking to like-minded parents about the evaporation of family time, the pernicious effects of the media, the takeover of family life by extra-curricular activities, and the actions of highly permissive parents of other teenagers.

James Levine, author and fatherhood advocate, has written about how he and his wife activated a community of parents when his daughter became a challenging teenager upon moving to a new school. The daughter's steadfast refrain was that "all the other kids" get to have more freedom, to have later curfews, and so forth. Jim and his wife called the parents of their daughter's five closest friends and invited them to meet for dinner at a Chinese restaurant. Jim reports that the result was an amazingly effective parent support group that met three times a year through their daughters' high school years. The group opened up channels of communication among the families, helped parents hold firm again sometimes unreasonable demands from their daughters, and helped their daughters resist unreasonable peer pressure. The parents held a joint graduation party for the whole group. Reflecting back on this experience, Jim's daughter told her parents that "It was comforting to know that all the parents cared about us. I felt scared a little bit about going to a new school and now I had not just my parents but my friends' parents sort of looking out for me."

I have recently joined with a group of parents and community leaders in a suburban Minneapolis school district to create a public awareness movement for taking back family time from our current hyperactivity. Our group, named "Family Life First," believes that the problem of lost family time is too big to be addressed just by individual families; it requires a community effort. We are committed to not blaming anyone or any group for the problem. Rather, we are fully committed to empowering parents to become confident leaders in family life, and to make judgments about balancing children's individual activities and family activities. We are naming the problem and seeking community support for solutions. Nowadays we must locate such communities and activate their common values in a society that is increasingly turning childhood into a time for individual consumption and parents into frantic providers of goods and services for children.

As parents, we are all in this struggle together. My wife and I survived the raising of our own children with our confidence and sense of community support reasonably intact. But I worry about how the consumer culture of today will affect my own children's parenting and the fate of my future grandchildren. I worry that I will sound like my friends who are already grandparents and who shake their heads at the timidity of their adult children as parents and the sense of entitlement of their much-loved and little-limited grandchildren. Indeed, we are all in this together, and the stakes are very high. Ours is an era where it takes personal courage and participation in a like-minded community to be a confident parent.

When you have found your courage and your community, then I urge you to be outspoken inside and outside your family. Tell your children about what principles you are following in raising them. Let your children know that family time and family rituals are very important to you, that chores are a time for children to give something to the family, and that parents should be parents and not buddies with their children. I have only recently realized that my wife and I did this with our children in the area of family rituals. We would talk about how important rituals like family dinner are to our sense of family, and the children picked up on these values and began to articulate them as well. I also remember discussions with our daughter Elizabeth, after she turned age twelve and began babysitting, about our philosophy of setting limits with children. She would say, with a wry smile, "So that's what you have been doing with me and Eric!" When you regularly let kids know why you do what you do—what your core values are—your decisions seem less arbitrary to them, even if they don't always agree with them. Confident parents can calmly articulate their values and explain their parenting practices to their children and to their wider circles of family and community. They go public with who they are and what they cherish about family life.

EXPECTING RESPECT

When my son Eric was about thirteen years old, we had a brief but memorable encounter in the kitchen, one of those moments which, like the road not taken, made all the difference for the future of our relationship. I was on the telephone with a friend in the early evening hours. Unbeknownst to me, Eric wanted to make a phone call to one of his friends. When I hung up the phone, Eric said to me, in an irritated, peremptory tone of voice, "Who was *that*?"

Do you agree with me that this was disrespectful behavior on Eric's part? If you don't see it that way, then, with all due respect, you need to read this chapter badly. Play out several possible responses I could have made, and then I'll tell you what I actually said.

Response #1 *(delivered in a mildly defensive tone)*: "I was on the phone with Mac. I didn't know you wanted to use the phone." The problem with this response is that it accepts the child's right to grill the parent about adult activities. The key is not the question itself, but the disrespectful demand. On the other hand, suppose I had been having an uproariously funny conversation on the phone, one that attracted Eric's bemused curiosity. It would have been perfectly appropriate for him to inquire, with genuine interest, "Who were you talking to on the phone, Dad?"

Response #2 *(delivered with mild reprimand)*: "I didn't know you were waiting to use the phone. You should let me know. How am I supposed to know?" This might be an appropriate response to a spouse or another adult peer who has equal rights to the telephone and is therefore free to express annoyance if you are clogging its use. Said to Eric, however, it would have accepted his offer of peer status, like a sibling whom he competes with for use of the shower or television.

Response #3 *(delivered with a stern reprimand)*: "Who do you want to call anyway? You are on the phone far too much. You should be doing your homework." This counterattack appears strong but misses the main point: the problem of the moment is not Eric's phone use but his disrespectful question. To simply assert parental authority over his phone use would make him resentful and would not teach him about this disrespectful action or forestall his next. What's more, it's likely to lead to an extended argument about his telephone use, an argument that masks the main issue at stake.

I've made my share of mistakes as a parent, but somewhere I learned (perhaps from my own parents) to have an instant awareness when one of my children is talking disrespectfully to me—and to make that the point of my response. So here's what I said, making eye contact and speaking firmly: "You don't get to ask me that question, and particularly in that tone of voice." The discussion was over. Eric absorbed my comment and then went to the other room to make his phone call. I did not name the person I was on the phone with. I did not defend myself. I did not counterattack. I did not make Eric defend his question. I did not punish him. What I did was to directly defend and assert my right to respect as a parent. And I did not feel angry at him during the rest of the evening. As a hormone-ridden, sometimes irritable adolescent, he had tried to invade parental boundaries, to turn me into a temporary peer whom he could vent at. I firmly declined his invitation, making it clear that I was the parent. Although during the subsequent years ahead we had the normal parent-adolescent hassles, he never spoke disrespectfully to me again.

If I had taken a different path that evening, one that would lead to similar encounters in the future, my son's adolescence and our family life might have been much different. When I work with parents whose children treat them disrespectfully, I always think of the story with Eric, and frequently share it. Mostly when I work with parents, however, the cat of disrespect is already out of the bag. The parents have permitted their child to be disrespectful, to invade the appropriate boundary of deference that separates the generations. In this chapter we will examine the signs of disrespect by children more thoroughly, so you can recognize it instantly.

Disrespect at Different Ages

Have you seen toddlers pounding, slapping, and kicking their parents? Outbursts of frustration are developmentally normal for two- to three-year-olds. But it is not developmentally normal for a parent to respond, as many now do, in the following manner: "Mommy doesn't like it when you hit her" or "It's not nice to kick people like that." Meanwhile, the child pounds away, ignoring the low-key prattle emanating from the parents.

There is a sad irony here. Many parents who want very much to raise their children to be respectful and non-aggressive actually encourage disrespect and aggression by their lack of vigorous response to their child's behavior. Citizenship starts when children are toddlers—both in the family and in the growing peer group. These young citizens have the right to not be treated violently and the responsibility to not be violent to others.

I remember a single mother, a politically active pacifist, whose son, age five, had started hitting and kicking her when he was angry. Committed to non-violence in her public life, she was appalled that she was raising a violent son, although he was not yet hitting other children. (He saved it for Mom, because his peers and preschool teachers would not tolerate it.) When she came to therapy, however, her stated goal was to be able to have heart-to-heart talks with her son the way they used to. I pointed out that it's hard to have heart-to-heart talks with someone who kicks you. I helped her focus on getting control over her son's aggressive behavior, and subsequently they returned to a warm mother-son relationship. Without respect, no sustainable warmth between a parent and a child is possible.

During the first six years of life, the template for later years is set down. This is also the time when the bogus psychology of "let them express their feelings" starts misleading so many parents. Jason, the four-year-old we discussed in the last chapter, developed the annoying habit of demanding his food. At dinner, he would shout, "Pour me milk!" or "Give me more french fries!" No one since King Henry VIII has gotten by with that kind of imperious behavior—the hired staff would quit.

At home, Jason had lost the skills of polite requests. It's not as if he had a disorder of impulse control, he was a model of appropriate behavior in preschool where the standards for politeness were clear and consistently enforced. How did Jason's parents respond? Often they tried to shut him up by immediately fetching what he demanded. Other times they got irritated with him and told him to ask nicely—but they still fetched his food without making him ask politely. Psychologists describe this as reinforcing the child's behavior.

Parents whose children treat them disrespectfully will eventually start to fear and resent their children. Parents will start withdrawing emotionally, or become punitive. They will have explosions of anger they feel bad about later. Or they will become sarcastic and passive aggressive. Ann, Jason's mother, felt badly about her lapses into sarcasm with her four-year-old. One evening, when Jason autocratically demanded more milk, Ann poured his milk with the dramatic gesture of a servant and delivered the following words in a sarcastic tone: "Right away, little Prince." In a flash, Jason retorted, "I'm not the Prince, I'm the King!" Ann was stunned—and disappointed in herself. Fight disrespect with disrespect and you will lose every time.

How did Ann and Paul turn things around with Jason's meal behavior? They firmly challenged him every time he asked for something rudely, and waited for him to politely restate his request before giving him the item. If he refused to ask politely, they withheld the food item and went about finishing the meal. Jason eventually learned the meaning of "polite," and the incidence of demanding behavior at table declined drastically. Ann and Paul did have to deal with the differences between themselves, however, since Paul was more likely to not recognize the disrespect. The parents were finally successful when they worked together as a team.

The importance of insisting on respect for yourself as a parent does not go away after your children grow up. Having college students or working young adults in the home presents lots of opportunities for renegotiating what respect means at this stage of the family life cycle. Let's say your twenty-three-year-old son is living at the family home in between jobs. You ask him to let you know his schedule for family dinners. Over and over, he fails to show up for a planned meal, only to blow off your complaints by saying, "Something came up. Don't worry, I'll eat the leftovers. What's the big deal?" Unless you deal directly with what you expect in terms of respect, you are going to become very negative towards him, or withdraw emotionally from him. At the very least, you want to be notified about cancellations of family events, and you probably want him to make a commitment to be part of family rituals. Disrespectful behavior also involves sins of omission—such as failing to do or say something expected—as well as sins of commission—such as verbal demands or direct rudeness.

When I was describing these ideas recently to a close friend, he told me something disturbing. His ten-year-old son is a polite, respectful child. For example, when asked if he wants a second serving at mealtime, he is apt to say, "No thank you. I've already had enough." Recently, he has been teased by adult relatives for his politeness with comments like, "Is that boy for real?" The boy cringes in embarrassment, not knowing what he had done wrong. Have our standards for children become so low that we now ridicule a polite, respectful child? I bet that the boy's behavior threatens his adult relatives, who have never expected politeness from their own children.

Strategies for Expecting and Getting Respect

The following are eleven key strategies I have used, and practiced, to establish a relationship of trust between parents and children. They should be used as guidelines—not as hard and fast rules—as you work to expect and get respect from your child.

1. Respect your child.

This is first and foremost. Children learn more by our actions towards them than by our verbal statements of values or expectations. Of course, nearly all of us believe that we respect our children, but sometimes we slip and get into negative patterns. Name calling is almost always disrespectful, even when done for "humor." I recall a teenage girl whose parents sometimes called her "lard ass" because of her weight problem. Reading kids' diaries is disrespectful, unless you fear grave danger—and then you should tell the young person what you did. Some parents use their children as gofers to wait on them. When you ask your child to do a favor, such as getting a soda pop for you, I think you should ask politely—"Would you be willing to get me a soda while you are in the kitchen?"—as opposed to ordering the child to do it. And they should have the right to decline doing us a favor.

Respecting children means giving them the psychological space to have and express their own opinions, tastes, and values, which are not really the objects of direct parental control. For example, ranting about teenagers' music tastes is insulting to them and their generation—and such disrespect diminishes our influence on their values.

Apologizing to our children is another powerful sign of respect. I recall a number of times when I told my children that, although I did not approve of their behavior that started the conflict—say, failing to do chores—nevertheless I was sorry for my reaction that was too strong. Beyond love, care, and protection, there is a bedrock of respect we owe our children, who are life's gift to us. Our children are not our possessions.

2. Expect respect.

Carefully evaluate the value you place on being treated decently by your children—and others in your life, for that matter. Although parental respect partly must be earned, mostly it is a right that comes with our humanity. Some version of the commandment to "honor thy father and thy mother" exists in all cultures. Disrespectful treatment of parents by children is a deeply disturbing trend in today's families. I urge you to begin thinking in terms of respect as a value in your family because without it, little else will go well.

3. Tune your ears to the frequency of respect and disrespect.

Many parents I see do not realize that their child is being disrespectful until I point it out. When a mother complains about the state of her fifteen-year-old daughter's room, the girl hisses back: "Yeah. Like your own room is not a filthy pigsty!" When a single mother tells her daughter she is concerned about some of the older boys she is hanging around, the daughter fires off this line: "They are no worse than that bozo you have been dating." Too many parents fail to recognize the sound of the disrespect in these exchanges because they focus too much on the content of what is said. Sometimes they get distracted by the fact that their child has made a partially accurate statement, say, about the bedroom or the boyfriend. Or, oppositely, they become enraged at the inaccuracy or unfairness of the child's counterattack. It's best to tune out the content (interruptions, accusations, and name calling) at these times and listen for the child's tone of voice.

A curse from a teenager should mean that the topic of the conversation is no longer the issue of the moment. It's not that you won't think about the content later—say, what does your daughter not like about your boyfriend—but for the moment, you must focus mainly on the insulting words and tone. Your "ear" has to distinguish between disrespect and legitimate frustration and anger. In the examples above, the teenager could angrily say, "I hate cleaning my room!" or "I feel like this is a police state!" This is anger, not contempt. A raised voice is not necessarily a sign of disrespect, but attacking, intrusive, and mean words and tone are. Gaining the skill to recognize disrespect is crucial for effective action.

4. Nip disrespectful behavior in the bud.

Respond immediately, if possible. Train your reflexes to act quickly. Say to your child, "That was disrespectful" or respond in another direct way to the impropriety of the child's comments. Don't walk away and fume about being talked to that way.

5. Cultivate a special tone of voice that communicates, "You are in dangerous territory; you would be wise to back off immediately."

I can't tell you how you can personally activate this tone of voice, but you likely know what I mean. It's the tone that says "Don't mess with me, buddy."

6. Explain your new policy on respect to your children at a quiet time.

Many children are unaware they are being disrespectful. After all, they have been allowed to get way with disrespectful behavior. Encourage your children to be allies in changing your relationship with them. When they sign up for the change, it goes much more smoothly.

Children are happier when they are consistently respectful to the most important adults in their lives. I coached parents to have a meeting to explain their new policy on respect with their eighteen-year-old daughter, who for many years had been hostile and nasty when angry, and generally intrusive at other times. For example, she would comment negatively on her father's weight and her mother's housekeeping. I pointed out to the parents that their daughter would probably carry over this pattern of behavior in her marriage and with her own children, and that they should consider changing the disrespectful dynamic for her own sake as well as theirs.

7. Focus on the disrespect, not on the content.

In your response, it is generally best to label and confront the child's inappropriate behavior without getting into the specifics of what the child is upset about. Imagine someone kicking you in the shins while asking to discuss the presidential election—you deal with the kicking and forget the politics for now. I recommend using terms such as "respect," "disrespect," "polite," and "rude." It is helpful in developing a common language, a word signal that the child can understand even when upset.

8. Use "time outs" for non-cooperation when the child will not cease the disrespectful behavior.

If a child is standing in the kitchen yelling rudely at you, first point out the disrespectful behavior in a firm voice. If the child does not relent, you can give a warning that there will be a time out enforced if they do not stop. If that does not work, then enforce the time out. By all means, do not allow a nasty conversation to proceed for very long: it's not good for you, your child, or the relationship.

A child who loses control emotionally and cannot calm down should be placed somewhere to cool off. With an adolescent, you might want to turn on your heels and remove yourself from the conversation, rather than trying to enforce a time out against physical opposition. The key is to declare yourself on the disrespectful behavior and abort the conversation rather than letting it escalate. Then have a follow up conversation later, when the storm has passed, listening to your child's feelings but insisting on respectful expressions of anger in the future.

9. Be firm but keep your cool.

If a child is out of control, it never helps for the parent to lose emotional control. Confident parenting is most always calm, clear, focused, and assertive in times of conflict. Some parents confuse being in charge with having repeated angry outbursts at their children. Such outbursts, rather than signaling that we are in charge, actually generate more disobedience and less respect from our children. Of course, we all lapse into hot anger at times, but it's worth trying to regain our composure quickly when we lose it. My daughter, Elizabeth, during a teenage moment of insight and openness, confided than she sometimes enjoyed seeing her mother and me get really worked up when we were arguing with her about her behavior. We vowed never to give her this pleasure again, and mostly stuck with our resolve.

10. Combine zero tolerance with a long-term view.

Remember, challenge every disrespectful behavior—without exception—because that is the only way that the child will understand your expectations and the meaning of the behavior you want to extinguish. But realize that a longstanding problem will not vanish overnight. If we as parents allowed our children to disrespect us, it behooves us not to get too self-righteous when it takes them time to learn a consistent new way to behave. Do not expect an immediate cessation of rudeness, but a steady decrease towards zero.

11. **If the problem is chronic and the preceding strategies don't seem to work, consider seeking family therapy to focus on your parenting skills.**

    Similarly, if you and your spouse (or co-parent) cannot cooperate and agree to a parenting style, consider getting help from a profes sional. Don't let the pattern go on for years to come.

When my son, Eric, went off to college, he told us how stunned he was about how a dorm floormate talked to his mother on the telephone, shouting such things as "Stop calling me so often!" and "Get your own life!" Eric noted that he would never "in a million years" talk to his own mother or father that way. That is how I felt about my own parents. I wish for all families that there be mutual and deep respect between the generations. As the leaders of our families, it's our job to give respect to our children and to expect it in return.

EXPECTING PARTICIPATION IN FAMILY LIFE

We are turning family activities—mealtimes, visits with relatives, vacations, and the like—into a consumer option for our children, not an expectation that comes with being part of a family.

If I am your sixteen-year-old daughter, why shouldn't I get to choose not to have dinner with my family? What if I am on the telephone in an important call to my friend about her breakup with her boyfriend? What if I don't like what you are cooking these days? What if I am not hungry? And how do you expect me to actually enjoy family dinner conversations dominated by my bratty kid sister?

Or suppose I am your eleven-year-old son who would much rather watch television reruns in the living room than sit at the family dinner table. When you make me join you in the dining room, I fuss about the food and generally make things unpleasant for everyone. When you let me leave with a tray to plunk down in front of the television in the family room, I am happy. Eventually, you stop expecting me to participate, although sometimes you try to cajole me into staying with the family.

Or imagine I am your four-year-old daughter, your only child, who hates to sit still for dinner. You spend a lot of your mealtime correcting me for getting out of my chair and being otherwise disruptive. Eventually, you give up and feed me separately before you have your own meal together as adults.

But you wonder when—and if—you will be able to pull off family dinner rituals. You worry that the family is missing out on something important.

In all of these actual scenarios from families I have worked with, the parents genuinely saw value in having family dinners together. They did not give them up without a struggle, but give them up they eventually did. Not because they were uncaring parents, but because they had become caught up in what I have labeled the consumer culture of childhood. They were unable to manage a child whose personal "consumer" interests did not include dining with the family. Just as in the market place, family life has become all about personal options and personal choice. As a provider of food services, the parents' main job is to put the food out and to provide the opportunity for a family meal. Given their reluctance to displease the child—the customer is always right in the consumer culture—how could they be expected to "force" their child to dine with the rest of the family. And, as in the three scenarios above, children increasingly punish parents who try to violate their zones of personal choice. It takes strong convictions and good parenting skills to hang tough.

In Minnesota, some people buy fairly affordable cabins in the plentiful lake areas, where for generations families have gone for vacations and occasional long weekends. There is lots of work involved in opening the cabin for the summer season, and closing it down in the fall. Family members spend a lot of time together recreating and hanging out around the lake and in the forests. It's a tradition for many families, such that the selling of the family cabin when parents become frail or die is a special loss of a tradition and its memories.

Young Minnesota parents considering buying a lake cabin nowadays are being warned by their older friends not to bother. Parents of teenagers assert that, while you can make your young children go to the lake for weekends and extended vacations, your preteens and teenagers will definitely refuse. Then you are stuck with a cabin you don't use. The sage counsel of these experienced parents is to rent a cabin while your children will still go with you, and plan to give up on most family trips and vacations later on when your children get their "own life."

Family Time and a Child's Own Life

Some involvement in activities outside of the family is desirable. It's only when they crowd out family time and family rituals that they become a problem. Later we will discuss the importance of children's school and community involvement, so please don't misread the intent of this chapter. If at the beginning of this century, children's primary life was supposed to be within the family, and secondarily in the school, and thirdly in the community at large, now we've reached the point where children's real life—their "own life"—occurs outside the home in a myriad of sports, music lessons, and other competitive and enrichment activities. The family becomes the launching pad on the carrier ship, with the real action occurring in the skies around the ship. The kids fly home to sleep and eat before taking off again. Parents become brokers of community services for their children, and they downplay the importance of face-to-face family time and family rituals such as meals, Sunday drives, vacations, and visits to relatives.

It's not that parents consciously choose to de-emphasize family activities. They give up their family time, one activity at a time, as their children get older and into more activities. When your children are young, even if you over-indulge them, you still will have lots of time with them—opportunities for important rituals such as after school snacks and talks, bedtime reading, and special trips to the ice cream store. When you visit relatives or take a vacation, of course your young children come along. To repeat: with young children, even if you lack balance between treating your children as consumers of services and citizens of your family, the danger to your family's sense of connection may not yet be evident.

But when your children get to the preteen and teen years, when their world has large doses of peer relationships and outside activities for them to "consume," you will lose your hold on your family activities unless you change course. You may not even notice for a while, since the erosion happens gradually. If your primary value is to help your children make their "own lives" as enriching as possible, and if you do not assert family togetherness as an equally strong value, then you will lose your family time and your family rituals. Simply stated, we either defend our family time or we lose it. The consumer culture of childhood is too strong to resist without a game plan and clear set of values.

The gradual nature of the loss of family time reminds me of what happens to frogs when they are put in a pot of water whose temperature is increased one degree at a time over several hours. The frog will simply stay in the water until finally it is too hot and dies. If you raise the temperature more quickly, the frog will sense the change and jump to safety. We are losing our family time one small decision at a time. We let our child sign up for a second sport in the same season and we say goodbye to weekends for the next six months. We let our teenager take a twenty hour per week job and we have said goodbye to family dinners. And we let the same teenager buy a television for the bedroom and we have said goodbye to being together in the family room during those rare times when we are home together. The loss of family time occurs one degree at a time.

What's So Important About Family Rituals?

Here's a mental exercise to try: Think about the warmest, most positive memories of your childhood. I'll bet the majority of them revolve around family rituals—the repeated, coordinated, meaningful activities of family life. My own memories go to family dinners, where my Irish storytelling father would hold forth and entertain us, and where I learned to tell stories myself. Also, I recall the vacations at the New Jersey shore and the picnic and swimming outings at French Creek State Park. Our Christmas Eve tradition of decorating the tree and throwing tinsel on the branches was also special. Like most people, I barely remember a single set of words my parents ever said to me, but I remember the rituals.

Surveys of parents testify that most parents believe that rituals such as family dinners are very important for children. And they are right. Research studies are beginning to document the benefits of regular family dinners for both young children and adolescents. The rituals themselves have an impact, but the quality and endurance of family rituals is a metaphor for the degree of family emotional connection. I have written extensively about family rituals in my book *The Intentional Family* (Avon paperback, 1999).

In addition to being good for children, what do rituals do for family life? Done well and faithfully, they are the glue of family life. According to researchers Steve Wolin and Linda Bennett, family rituals enhance family life in four ways. They are:

1. Predictability, a sense of order and regularity in family life;

2. Connection, a sense of emotional bonding;

3. Identity, a sense of being part of a specific, unique family;

4. Values enactment, a way to demonstrate in behavior what is important to the family.

Rituals are where the family's group culture is created and maintained, where the child feels part of something larger. In a ritual, each individual is temporarily caught up in a larger group activity, surrendering, for a short time, the demand to function as a solo actor. Rituals by nature are anti-individualist, which is why they are so threatened in contemporary American society and in families where parents are reluctant to "impose" family expectations on their children.

Children as Active Participants in Family Rituals

It's not enough to just *have* regular family rituals. Family rituals must include a sense of meaning along with only minimal conflict. Some families cease having family dinners because the conflict is too hard to take. In *The Intentional Family* I described ways to enhance the meaning of family rituals and to avoid unnecessary conflict. Here I will focus on an aspect of family rituals directly related to the theme of this book: children as active participants, that is, as producers of family rituals and not just as receivers or consumers of what is taking place.

From their earliest years, it is important to get children involved in shaping and putting on family rituals. Consider these examples of family dinner participation: A three-year-old cherishes the chance to blow out the candle at the end of dinner. A ten-year-old participates, in an age-appropriate way, in selecting the food for meals and helping prepare some part of the meal. Once a week, a teenager is responsible for the whole dinner ritual: menu selection, set up, cooking, and serving. The rule is that the parents do not criticize the teenager's efforts.

I know one family where the parents, after narrowing down the family vacation to acceptable options, turn the final decision over to a family meeting. Here children got to shape a very important family activity, and to learn about the importance of compromise. The discussions became a laboratory for working on their children's tendency to take an individual consumer stance: I want what I want, and reject anything else. Over time, the children learned that some years the decision goes one person's way and other years another person's way.

When our children were in their early teens, we always had difficulty in agreeing on what video to watch together. Neither child would agree to watch the video the other one picked. The art of compromise was missing, and no amount of adult lecturing could restore it. Our stopgap solution was to give them five minutes to come up with a joint decision, or we would choose the video ourselves. Sometimes one or the other child would refuse to watch the video that was eventually selected. In those days because we did not think of weekend video watching as a family ritual—although I now think it was—my wife and I would permit the dissatisfied child to stay apart from the family during the video. I felt bad about the child's absence, and frustrated.

Today, I think I would approach this video scenario differently. I would frame the weekend video watching as a family ritual if we jointly decided to do this activity that evening. (Usually, there was interest in watching a video as a family; the problem came later in selecting one. In fact, when we did it well, I have good memories of our family going through most of Alfred Hitchcock's movies over a period of months.) In other words, I would not impose the ritual on the children, but once they "signed on" to a family video night, I would expect that everyone watch it together even if they did not get to choose what we watched.

In another family, the grandparents take each grandchild on a trip to a destination of the child's choosing anywhere in the world when the child turns fourteen. (This family obviously has substantial means, but the principle is the same for less ambitious trip rituals that can take place within driving distance.) But isn't the teenager still in a consumer mode, a recipient of the grandparents' largesse? No, because the grandparents have the requirement that they and their grandchild first research possible destinations together. Once the child has chosen a spot, the three of them spend months studying about the country's history, culture, and attractions. The child is also expected to keep a daily log during the trip, and to share what he or she learned and experienced with the grandparents and other family members upon returning home. The child is an active shaper of a powerful ritual of connection with his or her grandparents.

Major religious rituals based in the family often have an important role for children. The Jewish Seder comes to mind. For families that celebrate Christmas rituals, there are many opportunities to help children be contributors to, not just recipients of, Christmas festivities. School age and older children can be brought into the discussion of what gifts other relatives might like to receive. And children can be given a specific amount of money to spend on presents for siblings and other relatives, along with coaching about how to think of the other person's needs and preferences.

There has been a lot written about rampant consumerism at Christmas, but one story stands out for me. A newspaper columnist described his guilt and embarrassment on Christmas morning, when his two children, upon realizing that they had not received the wildly popular Furby doll, broke into an demanding chant: "We want Furbies! We want Furbies!" Instead of being appalled, and dealing forthwith with this obnoxious and ungrateful behavior, the parents just felt remorseful. Their nine-year-old daughter later tried to buy a Furby doll from another girl at school, who was jacking up the price. The purchase was aborted only at the last minute by the other child's parents who thought that the uncle who gave the girl the gift "might" be offended if she sold it. Indeed, but is there not something else amiss with all the parents involved? A gift by definition is not something demanded, and not something to be sold to the highest bidder. But some contemporary children don't ask as much as demand—and their parents respond with guilt or excuses when they cannot meet their child's consumer demands at times of ritual gift giving.

But there are positive things to say as well. When we create spaces and expectations for children to contribute to family rituals, they usually come through. I met with a group of fifteen-year-olds to discuss family holiday rituals. I asked them to think of a favorite family Christmas ritual and how it benefited their families. Then I asked them a question that led to a fascinating discussion. The question was, "How do you contribute to this ritual?" I was not sure what I would get back from this question, or even if they would want to answer it. (During my opening remarks about the role of families in teenagers' lives, one vocal girl had proclaimed, "Families suck!") I asked the teens to break into small groups, and then we pooled their responses. The following is a partial list:

- Scheduling the neighborhood party before Christmas. One boy was in charge of calling neighbors and determining the best date for the annual neighborhood Christmas party.

- Another boy worked with his mother to make everyone's favorite traditional cookies.

- One girl treasured decorating the family tree with her mom.

- A boy enjoyed buying a "cool present" for his five-year-old nephew. He was proud of his ability to learn what a young child might want, and to get just the right present.

- One girl said that, during the sometimes boring time her family spends at grandma's, she contributes by talking with her grandma instead of just entertaining herself. She noted that many of her relatives do not talk with grandma like they once did because she repeats herself a lot.

- One boy took pride in cleaning the house before the big Christmas celebration and how the house looked when people arrived.

- Finally, one boy mentioned that he contributed to family rituals at Christmas by not "turning off" to a multitude of extended family members he didn't know well. This boy was able to let go of his normal teenage reluctance to engage with strange yet doting adults, thereby making the extended family ritual go better.

I was struck with these teens' obvious pride in their contributions to family Christmas rituals. Afterwards, one of the adults leading the youth program told me she had a revelation while listening to the teens. She always wondered why her family rituals with her own children collapsed after her divorce. What she realized by listening to the discussion was that her mother had done all the family rituals solo when she was a child, with minimum input from others. While she was married, the woman adopted her new in-laws' holiday and other rituals. After the divorce, she had no history—or skills—in creating and sustaining rituals. She realized that she had been strictly a consumer of family rituals, not a producer.

This story leads to another important point: Your children may react negatively and initially resist your efforts to engage them as active and regular participants in family rituals. Don't be deterred. Our children are being raised in a culture whose theme song is the legendary Frank Sinatra's anthem "I Did It My Way." You may have to make compromises; the family ship does not turn 180 degrees in a short time. And it's important to actively involve children in discussions about family rituals. But remember that as the family leader, you must think about the long term, not just the immediate struggle. Your children will eventually appreciate it when as adults, they understand how their active participation in rituals helped to form their sense of family.

The Importance of Family Work

Family life is not just about rituals and enjoyable activities. It is also about the work of maintaining the family dwelling and keeping family members fed and their clothes cleaned. Beginning when I was about age ten, I alternated doing the dishes with my older sister, a chore I did not enjoy and sometimes tried to get out of by sneaking out to play with my friends. I recall that never once did my parents do the dishes for me when I ran off. My chore was always there for me when I returned, usually after my younger sister retrieved me. In high school, I was also in charge of sweeping and mopping the kitchen floor every Saturday. If you had asked me, I would have said I hated that chore as well, but I remember now taking pride in doing a good job on the floor: removing all the kitchen chairs instead of working around them, rinsing the mop regularly so that it could absorb the most dirt, keeping everyone else off the floor until it dried. Doing the dishes and cleaning the highly-trafficked kitchen floor was part of my duty as a citizen of my family.

Some parents appear to feel guilty about requiring that children do some of the work of family life. Most children will not volunteer, or at least not stick with a chore without their parents' firmness. The result is half-hearted parental expectations for children's chores, lots of non-cooperation, and periodic battles. Eventually, some parents give up entirely, but resent their children's selfish attitude. This is a serious mistake, because we teach our children that they can get out of family work by skipping it and making life difficult for us when we protest.

The same children, when they reach the age of paid employment, may be models of responsibility in the work force: they show up on time, do their jobs well, and are pleasant to their bosses. (Of course, others carry their family behavior into the work place.) What is going on here? The difference is that employment serves the teenager's personal needs and goals—for a paycheck and increased consumption. Family work, on the other hand, has no immediate payoff for a child. It's an expenditure of time and energy without anything "back" except a sense of doing one's part. So it's not that our children can't or won't work, it's that they are reluctant to work for the family because of the consumer culture of childhood combined with parental ambivalence about what is to be expected of them.

Faced with their own uncertainty and their children's opposition, many parents resort to bribing children to do routine chores. I see nothing wrong with adding to a child's allowance when they have worked beyond the routine call of duty, but paying for regular family work like dishes and lawn mowing sends the wrong message. It confuses family work, which all family members have responsibility for, and paid work, which is a contractual relationship, a quid pro quo: I do this for my employer in return for money. At worst, it's a way to bribe children to do what they are supposed to do. Withholding payment then becomes a way to enforce the chore policy. But when youth get old enough to earn their own money, or when a younger child does not care much about money, this monetary carrot does not work.

When considering family work, it is important to distinguish between chores that contribute to the common good of the family—such as cleaning or picking up public spaces in the home—and chores that are mainly about self-maintenance, such as cleaning one's own room. After years of struggling with our children about the condition of their bedrooms, we finally decided to focus on family chores, not on their personal space. We let go of some of our expectations for neatness, on the basis that this was mostly their own issue and not worth the stress on our relationship with them.

However, we vigorously enforced other chores when they faltered at those.

The point is that I encourage you to consider the difference between your child's private domain and your child's contributions to the common domain in the family. Picking up the family room is family work. Making one's bed every morning is a private matter, at least for a teenager, and may not be worth battling over. At least that's how we resolved it. You may approach it differently.

Family rituals and family work are the two main areas in which we can expect full participation from children in family life. I urge you to raise your expectations—or at least confirm your current expectations—of your children. The key is to become an "intentional family" whose values are clear and is committed to its rituals and its common work. In a world that pulls families apart—degree by degree like the frog in the pot—only the clear-headed, confident parents will create the kinds of families they want their children to grow up in and contribute to.

WHY ANGER-FREE PARENTING DOES NOT WORK

To many parents, anger is one short step away from verbal and physical abuse of children. But anger is a normal human emotion that signals "something's got to change here—right now." Without anger, parents are wishy-washy in the face of their children's willfulness. In today's families, it seems as if only children have permission to get angry. Fear of showing anger to our children is at the heart of the impotence problem among contemporary parents.

Recently I observed the following too-common scenario: A boy (about age four) and his mother were walking on the beach. The boy ran ahead. He went under a fence and into a flower garden that was about six feet from a thirty-foot drop to the railroad tracks below.

As she approached her son, I heard the mother say to her son in a very mild tone, "Sweetie, I don't think it's a good idea for you to be back there." The boy stood and waited for her to arrive. Leaning over the fence, she put out her arm and said, "Jeffrey, come. Please get out of there. Those are flowers you are standing in, and you are too near the tracks." Motionless and defiant, the boy just looked at her. "Here, take my hand," she pleaded. Still no movement. It was clear that the child was enjoying this moment of stubborn victory.

As my wife and I continued our walk, I looked back for a while to see if there was any progress. The mother was leaning as far as she could over the fence and begging her son to take her hand, while he stared at her. I didn't wait for the ending. Perhaps the boy tired of the game. Perhaps the mother bribed him. Perhaps she threatened to punish him when they got home. Whatever happened, the child had learned another lesson in how to render a parent impotent.

Scenes such as this one point up the danger of anger-free parenting. Trying to remain cool and rational in a situation of defiance and danger makes us look foolish. No parenting expert would have supported the mother's pitiful pleading approach to this problem, but how would experts suggest she respond?

Thomas Gordon, author of *Parent Effectiveness Training*, would tell the mother to calmly deliver an "I message" such as "I get very scared when I see you standing there because it's dangerous." The assumption is that your child will spontaneously decide to cooperate if you express your true feelings. Gordon recommends never sharing angry feelings directly, because anger is a "secondary emotion." Since anger is a reaction to a primary emotion, such as fear, the primary emotion should be shared instead of the anger. Anger, in this way of thinking, is always dangerous to a child.

But what if your child is enjoying seeing you afraid? What if your son, like the boy behind the fence, is less interested in what he is currently doing than in displaying your lack of control over him? Sharing your vulnerable feelings is not going to get the job done in that case, although, in fairness, there are lots of situations when a well delivered "I message" is superior to barking orders at children. It's only a problem when something stronger is called for, as in the case of the boy in the flowerbed.

Another major school of parenting advice from the 1970s (written about extensively by Haim Ginott) would recommend a "consequences" approach. You would give your son an option: if he continues to stand there, he is choosing to accept a negative consequence you have promised. You could tell him that he will lose the ice cream treat you promised for the end of the walk unless he comes back under the fence. Or, you could inform him that there will be no more walks this week unless he cooperates.

Laying out consequences and waiting for the child to make a choice is a normal technique for effective parenting.

When your teenager won't do the dishes in a timely fashion, it's generally better to connect the chore with a consequence—say, no watching television or talking on the phone that evening—and let the child choose to cooperate. Continued non-cooperation means escalating consequences, until almost all kids will decide it's less hassle to do the dishes. That's a better approach, generally speaking, than standing over the child and forcing him or her to do the dishes.

A limitation of the consequences approach to discipline, however, is that it is not powerful and immediate enough for some situations. The defiant little boy in the flowerbed required a stronger response than the mother laying out the consequences of his continuing to stand there. In moments of willful confrontation, some children don't care about future consequences—they want things their way right now, thank you. In these situations, discussing future consequences rather than rising to the occasion comes across as weak.

What most of the rational, anger-free parenting advice misses is the importance of occasional angry power assertions by a parent. I say "occasional" because research has clearly pointed out that a rigid, authoritarian parenting ("I'm the boss; you be quiet and do what you are told") is counter-productive with children. It breeds anxiety and rebellion.

What do I mean by angry power assertion? In the case of the mother and her defiant boy, I would call him by name and say in a strong, loud voice: "Jeffrey, get out of there right now!" I would be moving towards him as I said these words. If he did not immediately move back towards the fence, I would shout "Come here!" as I arrived at the fence itself. If he did not instantly move towards me, I would climb the fence and retrieve him physically. Then I would get down face to face with him, and say something like the following: "I am furious at you. First, you went under a fence and into the flowers—and you know better. Second, you were near the railroad tracks—and you know better. And third, you did not come back when I told you too. You are in big trouble with me." I would take him home, with no further discussion. Later in the day, I would talk calmly with him about what happened on that walk, and what level of cooperation I wanted on walks in the future. I would expect him to agree to cooperate better in the future.

There are psychological levels deeper than what I have described, levels that could be explored after the original power assertion is successful. Perhaps the child's behavior, if it is unusual for him, reflects the stress of a recent family move. Perhaps he is angry at his mother about something. Perhaps he is testing his newly found four-year-old independence of his parents. On the other hand, if the behavior is chronic, then it also suggests a misalignment of authority between parents and child.

But whatever the deeper meaning of the boy's risky, defiant behavior, I must deal with the immediate situation. If you are stealing from me because of a troubled childhood, you have to first stop the stealing; then let's talk about your troubled childhood. Demonstrating hot anger is not a useful parenting practice in all or even most situations. It should be used sparingly; if overused, it creates a negative environment in the home and the children eventually tune us out. Angry power assertion is like the garlic in the salad: just the right amount does wonders, but too much overwhelms the rest. Some parents chronically overuse their anger. Others veer back and forth between too much anger and too much passivity. The pendulum has now swung so far that the new cultural problem is "anger phobia." We end up with bland parents who refuse to ever show anger to their children and subsequently lack power and allow their children to walk over them.

Why Some Anger Is Necessary in Parenting

All close relationships create friction, and none more so than parent-child relationships. We are such sources of frustration for our children that they need to be able to get angry at us—in respectful ways, of course. Most modern parents understand the importance of allowing their children to exhibit anger. It's displaying their own anger with their children that they have a problem with. Yet children are inevitably going to make their parents angry. If we don't express our anger directly to our children in constructive ways, we will take it out on them in some other way, such as using sarcastic humor, withdrawing affection, complaining about our children in front of them, or avoiding spending extra time with them.

In addition to the importance of expressing a normal human emotion, anger is sometimes necessary to get our child's attention when we are giving a directive. Psychologists have pointed out that the first step in changing a child's behavior is getting the child's attention. When your toddler is hitting you, she is not paying attention to your quiet statement that "Mommy doesn't like it when you hit her." Even if you are more direct, as in "Stop hitting me," you will not have the child's emotional attention if you say it too mildly. The message "Stop" must be accompanied with an emotionally engaging tone of anger in order for the child to have the chance to snap out of this behavior.

I like to observe people with their dogs. I now see the same kind of wishy-washy behavior among dog owners that I see with parents. The owner says, "It's not a good idea for you to be jumping up on these nice people, Sparky." Sparky is not listening, while the nice people are trying to fend the dog off. Dog owners are losing their ability to speak sharply and authoritatively to their animals, although that is exactly how obedience trainers say we should gain cooperation from animals. The result is out of control dogs that constantly irritate their owners and everyone around them. An out of control dog, like an out of control child, does not have a content disposition. It is not surprising that the Centers for Disease Control has reported a large increase in dog bites that require medical treatment, although the number of dogs has not increased in recent years. Dog experts point to two explanations: Owners are too busy to spend enough time with their dogs, and they don't know how to manage their dogs' behavior effectively. Hmm...sound familiar?

The final reason why a modicum of up-front anger is important in parenting is that it gives us the chance to show our children how to express this emotion constructively. If our children never see us express anger, from whom do they learn how to express their angry feelings in constructive ways? From their siblings? their friends? the media? They need to learn from us that anger is a natural emotion, that it serves a natural purpose without hurting anyone, and that it goes away. I know that this can be a difficult lesson to learn, especially if your own parents used anger in a threatening or abusive way, but it is important for our children that we find a middle ground between being nasty and being Casper Milquetoast.

It is important to model how to show appropriate degrees of anger for different situations. Parents who move from being completely calm to being a flaming madman or madwoman in an instant do not teach effective use of anger. Depending on the situation, constructive anger can range from irritation ("For the last time, pick up your toys before leaving the room"), to warm anger ("You are out of line talking to me that way, young lady"), to hot anger ("Get your butt out of that flower garden!"). Remember, parents who use hot anger all the time are often the most ineffective disciplinarians of all, because their kids eventually tune them out.

Parents who are not comfortable with the full range of anger expression, who feel guilty about even mild anger, teach their children that anger is wrong and that children are easily wounded by it. Sometimes, a very unassertive parent, like the mother of the boy in the flower garden, eventually blows up into rage, perhaps screaming uncontrollably at her child or even striking the child. Then, after calming down, she will feel terribly guilty, apologize to her willful son, and become more determined than ever to suppress all her feelings of anger in the future. This cycle of unassertiveness, rage, and guilt leads to chronic parenting problems.

How to Express Anger Constructively

Anger is like gasoline for a car. While anger is a necessary fuel for running parent-child relationships, it is also dangerous and explosive like gasoline and other fuels. Abusive anger destroys a person's spirit and sometimes his or her body. We have greater physical and psychological power than our children, and we have moral responsibility to use that power wisely. Perhaps no area of parenting calls for more wisdom than anger expression. Without enough expression of anger, we become impotent parents who teach our children that they are fragile. With too much or inappropriate expression of anger, our children will either be harmed or they will eventually dismiss us as chronic barkers.

Here are some guidelines I have learned for constructively expressing anger to children:

- Make eye contact with your child. Expressing anger while you are flailing around the room or lecturing into space does no good. Eye contact will help keep you focused on your child, and you will see his or her response right away.

- Make sure your words and non-verbal behavior are consistent. If you are irritated, your words and tone should both say "I am irritated." Be careful about inconsistency, as when a parent says "I'm upset with you," but does not look or sound upset. This is confusing for children.

- Never call your child names. Parents in past generations felt free to call their children "brats" or "dummies." Name-calling does not change a child's behavior, and it can do harm over the long run if the child takes to heart a negative label. When we name call, we stoop to the level of a playmate rather than staying at the level of a parent.

- Speak personally. Use "I" expressions. Avoid third person namby-pamby expressions like "Mommy doesn't like it when you throw things." Avoid bringing up another party with comments such as "Your father will be very upset with you." The anger at the moment is yours, not somebody else's, and the child needs to know that. Say "I am angry (mad, upset, frustrated, furious)." Using "I" statements also helps prevent negative attacks on the child's personality, such as saying, "You are a brat."

- Do not expect the child to immediately apologize or say much at all. When I am angrily asserting my parental power, I am not looking for negotiations at that moment. I am taking over the discussion. Avoid angrily asking "Why did you do that?", because often children don't know why they misbehave, or they won't tell us even if they do know. Expecting an immediate explanation or apology is a command that you cannot enforce and that may be unfair to the child at that moment. Expect behavioral compliance at such moments, not apologies or any other words. Words can come later.

- If an angry scene is upsetting to you or the child, talk about it later when everyone is calm. Do not apologize for your anger if it was appropriately delivered, even if the child was upset by it. If your anger was excessive or disrespectful, then do apologize for that element of it. But avoid a blanket policy of apologizing for yelling at your children, because often the child will know that the hot anger was well-deserved and will feel confused by your apology. One recent parenting handbook suggested that a parent who has gotten angry tell the child later on that "I am sorry for getting angry at you, but your behavior was really out of line." I think this is a mixed message and it implies, falsely, that the children's behavior forced me to use hot anger.

- Finally, avoid getting back into your anger in the debriefing discussion with the child; the point now is to learn from what happened in order to avoid the need for these confrontations in the future.

When Not to Express Your Anger

Don't take the bait if you sense your child is looking for you to get angry. Sometimes children know when to push our buttons, and we are better off responding with great cool—but still be in charge. Do you remember little Jason from the first chapter—the "king" of his family? Well, the parents did a good job of gaining control over his tendency to order them around. But the mother reported that she could not get Jason to stop calling her a "dummy" in the car when she would not stop for refreshments. The mother would respond with moderate anger, informing him that this was not respectful. Jason would keep it up—"dummy, dummy, dummy"—whereupon the mother would threaten consequences (such as grounding him to his room) when they got home. But Jason didn't care about this consequence; in fact, he liked to spend time in his room when he got home. And the mother was not sure what other consequence to apply.

I suggested to the mother that she see Jason's "dummy" as a four-year-old expression that she could choose to not take all that seriously. (I remember my five-year-old son threatening me with a classic line that works so well among his age group, "I won't be your friend." To which I responded, "Fine.") Instead of predictably responding with anger and limit setting, the mother decided to rise above Jason's put down with humor. In the future, when he called her a dummy, she simply said, in a light tone of voice, "I guess you're right. I must be a dummy." This response dumbfounded Jason, who before long gave up saying this word to his mother.

The point of this story is that we are not robots who must always respond in predictable ways to our children's transgressions. Sometimes a calm but firm response is better than a hot response, and vice versa. Calm can be as strong, if your non-verbal behavior shows strength. In fact, sometimes in really serious situations—say, your teenager took the car without permission and totaled it—it is better to maintain complete calm and refrain from direct expression of anger until the emergency is passed.

When I was about twelve years old, I vividly remember throwing my sister's eyeglasses holder at her, only to discover that her glasses were in it. The glasses shattered against the wall, and my sister charged upstairs to alert my parents. I had never broken anything that important before, and I was mortified. And it was only partly an accident—I had chosen to throw the holder, after all. To my everlasting gratitude, my parents remained calm and made immediate plans to replace the glasses. They could see that I was frantic with guilt and shame. I knew we didn't have a lot of money in our family, and that my sister really needed those glasses to see. There was no need for my parents to pile on with long-winded reproach. And I never, ever, threw anything at my sister again. If I had been making excuses, on the other hand, I imagine my parents would have reprimanded me with well-deserved anger.

For people who have too many bad memories of their own parents' nasty anger, expressing anger at their own children can be difficult terrain to navigate. In the therapeutic culture of parenting, anger is seen as inherently harmful to children. Expressing anger is a throwback to the bad old days of authoritarian parents and mean teachers. And in the consumer culture of childhood, we must make our children satisfied customers and happy campers. You can see why expressing anger to their children is so difficult for contemporary parents. But, in truth it is not impossible if you allow yourself to feel the anger, if you don't try to talk yourself out of your feelings once you have them, and if you use common sense guidelines for constructively expressing your anger. Used appropriately, anger becomes a necessary but temporary thunderstorm passing through the family, followed by much clearer air and the opportunity for making a better relationship between parent and child.

Building the Village: Responsibilities to School and Community

You've likely heard the oft-cited African proverb that "it takes a village to raise a child." I think the reverse is also true, that it takes a child to raise a village. Without children to nurture into productive citizens, a full human community would be impossible to imagine. And unless we involve our children in building the village, the community itself will be lost when their generation reaches adulthood.

What do I mean here by village or community? I mean schools, neighborhoods, religious congregations, clubs, teams, political organizations, volunteer organizations, and other similar groups. A village, or community, is all the groups outside the family that are not in the workforce sector. In the community you are productive, you contribute to the common good, but you are not paid for your efforts. The rewards come from the participation itself and from the sense of building the community.

We are seeing today an urgent concern about building and maintaining community. There is a widespread sense that we are too isolated from one another, too distrustful of those around us, too cut off from sources of support. Indeed, over the past thirty years, there has been a decline of public faith in every major institution in American society, from schools, to government, to religion. And there has been a decline in civic participation as well, with fewer people joining the social and service organizations (for example, the

Lions Club and the PTA) that once gave backbone to the community.

What does participation in these types of community organizations have to do with parenting? The older our children get, the more they are shaped by their community environment and the less they are shaped by us as parents. In certain areas, parents doing a heroic job one-on-one with their children often fail when the neighborhood is gang infested. A teen's quest for popularity and social status among peers can overwhelm the best efforts of parents to teach more appropriate values.

We all know that a school will play a crucial part in a child's development. Many of us also seek out churches and synagogues to help teach our children religious values. Community youth leagues offer children the opportunity to learn and participate in team sports. Without a doubt, children are receivers of vital community services. But in this chapter I want to emphasize the "other side" of community in the lives of our children: that is, our children's duties and responsibilities to their communities. Remember, children are not only consumers of community, but are also builders of community.

School as Community

Outside of the family, the school is the primary laboratory for the development of children as citizens. Unfortunately, our society has come to see the school as a service center for children and families, and children mostly as consumers of these services. They are consumers of teaching services, of school activities, and of facilities and equipment. As parents, our job is to select the schools with the best services and then make sure our children take full advantage of them. It was not always this way. The public schools were founded with a profound vision of building democracy through community commitment to universal education. The educated citizen would be actively involved in democratic self-government. Most private schools were also founded upon strong values about citizenship and community. When schools become just educational service centers, rather than seedbeds of active citizenship, we lose part of the soul of a democracy.

Teachers and school administrators are increasingly nervous providers of educational services. They feel blamed for declines in children's learning and test scores, for discipline problems, for the lack of safety in school. They are afraid to exercise firm limits with children because of how parents might respond. If forty years ago when I was a child there was too much automatic parental endorsement of school disciplinary decisions—the teacher or principal was always right—nowadays it's often the reverse. If my child is in trouble, someone at school has messed up. If a child is suspended, parents show up at the first meeting with an attorney. Regulations designed to protect individual children's rights sometimes endanger other children and teachers. A worried high school teacher lamented a law that allows a child who is expelled from one school (but not jailed) for violence against a teacher to be admitted to any other school in the district the next day.

Experienced teachers have seen big changes in the attitudes of students and parents just in the past ten years. Two first-grade teachers told me that children now try to give them orders, such as "Pick up my pencil!" after the child has dropped it on the floor. Does this sound like our discussion of entitled children and servant parents? Other teachers say that parents now assume that the school has done something wrong if their child is not learning well enough or is getting into trouble. When these parents come to family conferences to discuss the problems, they assert or imply that the problem lies in the school, not the home, and that it's the school's responsibility to fix it.

This reminds me of the Doonesbury cartoon in which a child is showing his report card to her father. The father says, "These are very poor grades." The girl replies, "I know it, Dad." In the last panel, the father says sadly, "I am very disappointed in your teacher." The girl replies, "Me too, Dad."

In one private school I know, a new policy has been put into place: parents may not send the nanny as a substitute for parent-teacher conferences, and nannies may not substitute when parents have volunteered time in the classroom. When

I heard about this shocking nanny rule, I saw it as the logical outcome of seeing children as consumers and parents as providers: parents can feel free to "outsource" the services.

Child psychotherapy services are quickly moving in this direction. Therapists refer to "drive by sessions," in which the parent drops the child off at the clinic, runs errands while the therapist "works on" the child, and is unavailable to meet with the therapist during the session. You drop off your car, don't you? It's the mechanic's job to fix it. Can you also see how these parents, who probably feel guilty for neglecting their children, are incapable of saying "no" or otherwise displeasing their child? They raise children who are over-serviced, under-nurtured, and out of control.

Not only are schools influenced by the consumer culture of childhood, they are also caught up in the same therapeutic culture that affects parents. The most important thing is not that children learn and become good citizens, but that they feel good about themselves. Thus children are given social promotions rather than face the consequences for their failure to learn. (In fairness, sometimes the failure is the school's fault as well.) Parents worry more about the impact of academic failure on their child's self-esteem than about why their child may not be working hard enough to succeed. Of course, there are children with genuine learning problems, but even they must be challenged to work to their capacity.

Psychologist William Damon tells a story reported to him by one of his students who took a teaching job in an ethnically-diverse school in New York City. She began to get complaints from parents about how much math she was doing in class and how much math homework she was expecting. Despite her best efforts to reassure the parents that she was offering developmentally appropriate math instruction, the complaints increased. Befuddled, she met with the school principal, who told her that these complaints were voiced commonly from parents from one ethnic group. These parents contended that since their children were on the average not good at math, it hurt the children's self-esteem to be exposed to too much math instruction. Fortunately, the principal supported the teacher in continuing to have appropriately high expectations of all the children in her class.

The schools have their own share of responsibility for problems in education. In the past, they did not try to involve parents enough. School professionals too often implied that the community should trust the teachers and stay out of the way. Schools have become rigid bureaucracies. Some teachers have responded to public distrust and to union protections by lowering their standards and just getting by. But some school leaders are coming to grips with these problems and really trying to turn the schools into places of community participation and active citizenship. And teachers are the primary community resources, outside of families, for developing the next generation.

Our Duties to School

Let's start with our duties as parents to the school. If we are to be more than family consumers of school services, we owe it to our own children, to other children, to the teachers—indeed, to the whole village—to actively participate in school community. I stress here that this commitment has to go beyond our stake only in our own children's education. If schools are to work, we must care about *all* the children. If another child is a source of disruption in a classroom, I have to see that child as more than a negative influence on my child's learning, but as a kid in need of help. I have to care about teachers and programs that my own child will never encounter, because I cannot separate my child's welfare from that of other children in the community.

What does caring for school community involve? It starts with showing up at every school meeting for parents. It means getting to know my child's teacher, paying careful attention to the curriculum, monitoring my child's work, making sure my child's homework is done, sharing in projects and learning activities, spending time volunteering in the classroom and on field trips, giving positive feedback to the teacher and other school professionals when I see things I like, letting them know promptly when I have concerns, and working collaboratively when problems arise. It means getting involved in the local parent/school organization, working on action projects with other parents, and participating politically by supporting school board candidates whose values I support.

Not surprisingly, many years of research have found that this kind of parental involvement in school is one of the main contributors to children's academic success. When we give generously to community, our own children inevitably benefit. As President John F. Kennedy used to say, "A rising tide lifts all the boats." When we help our child's school improve, it helps everyone's kids, including our own.

What about our children's responsibilities to their school community? Most discussions of children's work ethic in school focuses too narrowly on how the child will benefit personally from studying and working hard. Of course that is a valid consideration: the work habits learned in school tend to last a lifetime, for better or worse. But the downside of making school responsibilities strictly an individual matter for the child is that it misses the dimension of social responsibility.

What do I mean? Each child in school is a member of a learning community. As a citizen of this community, each child has rights and responsibilities. The rights include having a competent teacher, a good curriculum, adequate facilities, and a social environment conducive to learning. The responsibilities include showing up on time, cooperating with the teacher, doing one's work, and behaving in a way that creates an environment conducive to everyone's learning.

I realize that this list of responsibilities has nothing original in it. But I think that the emphasis today is usually on the students' responsibilities for their own learning, plus not getting in the way of others' learning. For example, "Study hard and you will get good grades, which will help you go to college" or "Participate in extra-curricular activities so you can enjoy high school, develop your potential, and have something on your resume for college."

But what about an additional set of reasons for acting responsibly in school? When a teacher assigns homework, is this not a social contract with the students? My child's teacher is expecting the work to be done and turned in. Simply stated, my child owes it to the teacher to follow through. My child also owes doing the homework to the other students, because my child will not be a good partici-pant in the group learning process tomorrow if the home-work is not done tonight. Not doing the work lets down the whole learning community.

The advantage of thinking in terms of children's respon-sibilities to their school community, not just in terms of their individual self-interest, is that it can help parents hang tough when our children don't see any personal benefit in doing school work. When a child is reluctant to do math homework because "it's boring and I'm never going to use it anyway," parents can only fall back on the consequences of not turn-ing in the assignment: "You will fall behind in math" or "Your grades will go down."

Falling behind and getting bad grades are valid concerns. But I suggest we can also add citizenship and social responsi-bility to the reasons for students to do their best work possi-ble. The teacher and other students are expecting my child to do his or her work, even if it is boring and hard. As a citizen of this classroom, my child has responsibilities to be an active contributor to the learning community.

I grant you that this is pretty idealistic stuff. It would require quite a shift in thinking from our current educational environment, which focuses on teachers as providers and children and families as consumers of professional services. Consumers have responsibilities to no one except them-selves—to cut the best deal—whereas citizens must consider the common good along with self-interest. But if we are to move past the current culture of mutual complaint between families and schools—the debate about which is more responsible for inadequate education—then I think we have to view schools as communities of learning which require the mutual responsibility of all involved.

Responsibilities to a Religious Congregation

For most families, participation in a religious congrega-tion is a principal source of community involvement. Research has demonstrated that families that participate in a religious congregation have lower divorce rates, improved psychological health, and better adjusted children. For families with children, churches (I will use this generic term here to mean all religious congregations) are one of the only community structures that includes members of all generations, from young to old. In an increasingly secular world, religious communities are a place where transcendent values are taught and aspired to.

Unfortunately, churches have not been immune to the consumer culture. They are running as scared as parents and schools. I hope you will permit me a bit of a tirade here. Churches are increasingly seeing themselves primarily as providers of a variety of market-driven services for members, starting with worship services that are expected to be engaging, interesting, and without challenge. Sermons are far briefer than in years past, in order not to tax the attention spans of the television generation. Sermons are also to be non-controversial, lest anyone be offended. A minister I know gets annoyed when parishioners say they are "offended" by something he said, not with the expectation of further dialogue, but with the expectation of an immediate apology from the pastor. Implicit is the notion that the preacher's job is to inspire but not make anyone uncomfortable. If you think of provider-customer relations, when a customer is offended by something the provider has done or said, the provider is trained to apologize and make things right. So much for prophetic vision in the pulpit.

The most successful (that is, fastest growing) contemporary churches offer much more than dynamic, engaging worship. They have well-developed pastoral care services, programs for young children, youth, singles, and seniors, study groups, divorce support groups, book groups, and loads of other services for special interest groups. All of this is good—I am not knocking churches for offering an abundance of services and ways to become involved. But church professionals can get so good at programming that members are able to participate cafeteria-style, selecting from the menu rather than building the beloved community. These congregations hold together as long as the clergy leaders keep the worship services engaging and the consumer opportunities fresh, because today's consumers of religion are committed less to denominations or even to congregations than to having a good experience.

Like schools and families, churches have also been profoundly influenced by the therapeutic culture. In many ways, this has been a positive development, as pastors have moved away from an excessively negative emphasis on human frailty, based frequently on an inadequate knowledge of psychology. God's love is now preached more than God's wrath, and someone seeking pastoral counseling is more likely to encounter compassion than harsh judgments or rote recitation of Bible passages. But, for me, too many clergy now teach a religion that sounds like warmed-over humanistic psychology: the goal in life is to pursue one's personal goals and passions, guilt is a barrier to an authentic life, and social conformity interferes with true spiritual growth. A church in Southern California proudly displays its name typifying this new style of religion: The Fellowship of Self-Realization.

Popular religious leaders and therapists now focus more on "spirituality" than on "religion." Spirituality usually refers to something private and personal—an individual's very own spiritual sense. Religion refers to the group and institutional domains, which are out of favor with those walking their own spiritual path. Unfortunately, spirituality stripped of religion—of tradition, of community structures, and mutual accountability—becomes just one more item in the shopping cart of the consumer culture. A sociologist once interviewed a therapist named Sheila who said she practices the religion of "Sheila-ism."

As homes for the consumer and therapeutic cultures, churches unwittingly do nearly as much as youth sport's programs to erode family time and family rituals. Most church programs are geared to individuals, not to families. The irony for religious families is that the more they are involved in their church, the less they see one another. Family dinner rituals and bedtime talks give way to church meetings. Attending Sunday school activities and adult Bible school classes means that the whole family is never together at one worship service. Youth programs take teens away on weekday nights and weekends. Committee meetings mean that the parents do tag-team parenting in the evening.

It can be different. In a small town in Minnesota, a group of adults and youth was formed to work on a common project. At the end of their October meeting, they tried to find a second time to meet. Nothing was available until January, and the young people's schedules were more packed than the adult ones. The group realized that church activities were the main culprit. They proceeded to organize a discussion in their church community about family time. The result was a decision that all church activities would be held on Saturdays, Sundays, and Wednesday nights—no exceptions. If you are in two groups that each meet Wednesday night, then choose one. It was a remarkably brave decision.

Okay—my ranting about churches is over. What does this have to do with you as a parent? My point is similar to the one I made for schools. Churches are places where children and families can participate in building the village—or, in religious terms, God's kingdom. For parents, this starts with the decision of whether to expect your children to participate in worship, religious education, and the coming-of-age rituals such as confirmation and Bar and Bat Mitzvah. From a child-as-consumer perspective, you should only take your children to these activities only as long as the children are enjoying them. But chances are that at some point in middle childhood, your children would rather do something else than go to church or other religious activities. They will start to complain about boring classes or adult-oriented worship services. They will make life miserable for you every week.

If religion is not particularly important to you, then you will have trouble insisting that your children continue to participate when they escalate their consumer complaints. And if you don't participate yourself in the religious community, you will annoy church leaders and teachers if you engage in "drive by" religious education for your children: drop them off and head for the coffee shop. My advice is to not expect your children to participate in something that is not especially important to you. There are other forms of value-based community you can choose for your family.

But if religion is a high value for you, then I suggest that you not give your children the power to remove themselves from it. If participation is not an option, but an expectation, most children will settle into the routine without too much fuss. It's when they see the door partly ajar that they kick at it persistently. On the other hand, if the children's programs are inadequate or poorly administered, then you should work to improve them rather than just requiring your children's attendance.

The best religious activities for children are those that get them involved in the enactment of community and religious values—as contributors not just as passive recipients of religious knowledge. This can be as simple as developing vehicles for children to communicate back to their families and other adults what they are learning about their religion. It can involve service projects for the church and for the wider community. And best of all, in my view, it can involve projects that the whole family can engage in together, projects that visibly contribute to the religious community and to the village beyond.

I have always been impressed by the Jewish Bar Mitzvah and Bat Mitzvah rituals. They beautifully combine personal learning and growth for the child with a ceremonial activity that the child plans and delivers for the benefit of the family and wider community. After an intensive year of absorbing the larger Jewish heritage, the child emerges as someone who can speak to others about that tradition, who can credit parents and others for their contributions, and who can inspire everyone with a speech on a biblical text. The child has become not just a consumer of Judaism, but a contributor to the tradition.

Other Ways to Link Children With Community

There are lots of ways to contribute to community as a family beyond school and church. My friend Patrick coordinates a block party each year in his St. Paul neighborhood. He gets his two children and other neighborhood families involved from the outset in the planning, and they are important assistants in pulling off this community-building event. His leadership speaks more to his children about community than any set of spoken values.

Another family I know makes their decisions for charitable financial giving as a whole family. Annually, the parents and school-age children review where they gave money the last year, and examine new ideas for giving that have emerged during the year. When they are considering giving to a community program, they do research on it. They ask for written information, which they discuss as a family. When they have narrowed the list, they visit these places so they can learn more about them firsthand. And after they have made their choices and promised the money, they choose one of the settings to volunteer in as a family. The parents have created a laboratory for community involvement for their children, who I suspect will be community builders their whole lives. How much better than if the parents simply wrote checks each year.

I will end this discussion with a difficult topic: the responsibilities of parents and children as citizens in the political community. It is difficult because so many parents are turned off to politics and government, and communicate this disenchantment to their children. The voting rates for eighteen- to twenty-four-year-olds have been declining in every election since eighteen-year-olds were allowed to vote in 1972. This group's voting rate for mid-term elections is now down to fifteen percent. Does this alarm you? Something is happening in our culture—and in our families—to discourage our youngest voters from exercising their fundamental responsibility as citizens.

I suggest that we owe it to our children to pay attention to the public world of politics and citizenship. Children learn from us what is important in the larger world. Sharing our views of political events, and encouraging our children to develop knowledge and opinions, helps grow citizens who will care about their communities. When you vote, do you talk about it with your children? Do you tell them whom you voted for, and which election issues were important to you? My father, with his passion for following the news and his willingness to express his opinions and values forcefully, left me a legacy of interest in the civic world that I carried over with my own children. I remember telling my children, after almost every election, that I felt a "rush" when I entered the voting booth. For me, voting is partaking in a sacred sacrament of democratic citizenship.

When your eighteen-year-old approaches his or her first opportunity to vote, I encourage you to talk up the election and make sure he or she is planning to vote. But aren't they adults now? Shouldn't we avoid pressuring them about their own adult decisions? I believe there is nothing wrong with applying some pressure to one's young adult children to do the right thing by voting, and with letting them know you are disappointed if they do not vote. And I expect them to do the same for me if they see me shirking my civic responsibilities.

Beyond voting, children benefit if they see their parents engaged in the political world as concerned citizens who attend public meetings, meet the candidates, and help with political campaigns. On the other hand, if parents too freely share their cynicism about the dishonesty of all politicians and the corruption or inefficiency of all levels of government, children will avoid the political domain of citizenship. I am not arguing for pretending that we think all is well with politics and government. But a single-minded emphasis on what is wrong, coupled with no visible efforts on our part to make things better, leads only to disenchantment and civic disengagement on the part of our children. These young people who do not vote—they are our children. We can do better by them so that they do better for us all.

There is an Irish saying that we take warmth from fires we did not build and we drink from wells we did not dig. We owe a debt to the community that raised us and sustains us. Parenting our children is not a solo act. As the village goes, so go our children—and as the children go, so goes our village.

CONFIDENT PARENTING IN TWO-PARENT FAMILIES

If you are in a two-parent family, you know the advantages of having another committed adult to support you in raising your children. You have someone at hand to talk things over with, to share decision making, and to help shoulder the labor of raising a family. Your children have a model of adults working together for the good of others.

You also know what can go wrong when two parents don't raise children as a team. Two parents pulling in different directions have a harder time raising responsible children than one competent parent by himself or herself. Two-parent families are usually the best environment for children to grow up in, but two-parent families can also be a poor environment for raising children if there is poor cooperation between the parents.

You might think that close cooperation between parents is an obviously good method of parenting. But a curious idea has recently entered some family discussions of parental teamwork. I will describe it through the family of Sarah, a typical fourteen-year-old girl who is the only child of two loving parents. Sarah prefers to negotiate with each parent separately for privileges such as going to the movies and having weekend overnights with friends. Like other smart teenagers, she looks for which parent is more permissive on these decisions. Her parents, however, are appropriately cautious about how much freedom to give her at age fourteen, and they generally check with each other before making a decision.

So far, the story is a familiar one: a child wants to maximize her freedom by getting permission from the parent she thinks is more "open" to her new experiences, and the parents close ranks and resist her efforts to divide and conquer. This scenario is probably as old as families themselves. What is new is that Sarah openly complains about being "ganged up on" by her parents, and the parents feel a touch of guilt for outnumbering her and outmaneuvering her.

When I first heard about these complaints from children, I was puzzled. How could anyone think that two parents working closely together constitute an unfair advantage over their own child? Of course, if the parents make poor, unfair decisions, then that's another matter. But Sarah was complaining about the unfairness of the parents' teamwork itself, not just the direction of their decisions. When I heard that the parents basically agreed with her—expressing regret about having to gang up on her, and understanding that this must be difficult for her—I was befuddled.

Here is how I interpret this kind of thinking: children increasingly want to relate to their parents as peers. Although children have to accept the reality that their parents have more power than they do—and hence are not fully peers— they can at least believe that they should have a major say in every decision that affects their well-being and desires. If Sarah is directly negotiating with both parents, and they don't talk with each other outside of her presence, then at least she has the idea that she is a full partner in the final decision.

But when the parents discuss matters behind closed doors and come to an agreement, contemporary children, especially teens, are apt to see this as inherently unfair. It throws in Sarah's face the power imbalance in the family. Why should her parents have their own private decision-making discussions that she is not privy to? How can she make her best case if she is not present for the debate? It's so unfair.

To better understand this situation from Sarah's perspective, imagine that you have two roommates with whom you must negotiate decisions about your shared household. After you have deliberated with each of them separately, you find out that your roommates get together without you, make the final decisions, and then take a united front in your presence. Foul play! You have the right not to be ganged up on by your peers.

It's bad enough that many of today's children feel entitled to be part of every discussion their parents have about them, but it's worse when their parents feel ambivalent about exercising proper parental teamwork. Sarah's father tells his friends that he can empathize with his daughter's feelings of being ganged up on, because, after all, there are two parents and just one child. You know, two against one. He thinks that if Sarah had a sibling, she would feel less unequal.

I challenged this father on two counts. I contended that parents owe it to their children, and to each other, to work closely together. That's the job of parents—to be a team, including making decisions during private conversations. Of course the decisions will be better ones if the parents have thoroughly discussed them with the child, whose wishes and feelings must count. But there is nothing remotely unfair about parents talking in private and thereby acting like parents. The father's empathy was misplaced, as was his guilt. That fact that Sarah felt the way she did was the problem; the parents' behavior was not the problem. It is misplaced empathy to feel badly for a child whose parents are acting like parents should act.

The second point I discussed with the father was the idea that their daughter would feel less ganged up on if she had a sibling. Most of the controversial decisions we make for our children are made for one child at a time—whether to allow a new sports activity, a sleepover, a concert. The presence of a sibling does not much affect the child's feeling of being outmaneuvered by the parents on these matters. It's not as if your younger sister is going to fight for your right to a later curfew than she has.

Sarah's parents seemed to be making good decisions and exercising appropriate control. But, in being unnecessarily apologetic about Sarah's feeling of being ganged up on, they are missing the opportunity to teach her about how two-parent families work. They are failing to remind her of the difference between being a parent and being a teenager. Instead, they implicitly endorse the notion that no two family members should have leverage on the third. One for all, all for one—except that the children will end up being only for themselves because they are not mature enough yet.

How does this pattern affect children's sense of respect and responsibility, their citizenship in the family? Uncertainty about the legitimacy of parental teamwork inevitably leads to confusion among children about what is appropriate to say and do to parents. A sense of entitlement to treat parents as peers will gradually creep in. Sarah, who has only a mild case of peer entitlement at this point, does feel free to lecture her parents about how her era is different from when her mom and dad grew up in. She is pushing the envelope of respect for her elders.

Sally, as a teenager, was farther along. Her behavior was often a challenge, she openly criticized her father for being out of shape, and her mother for being a sloppy housekeeper. Her parents had never successfully controlled her tongue, and when, on the rare times they met privately to try to set down some new rules for her behavior, Sally would turn her fury on them for "talking behind my back." When I coached the parents on acting like a team, Sally at first objected strongly that this was unfair. But when the parents confidently held their ground, she became a happier and more cooperative young person. Most kids really do appreciate it when their parents work together with confidence.

Children feel more secure when their parents are a team. It is a scary thing for children to have too much power in their own upbringing, especially the power to divide parents. This insecurity will show itself in lack of respect for parents. It will also show itself in conflicted peer relationships, romantic relationships, and student-teacher relationships. I have heard recent graduate students object to the procedure whereby the faculty meet to evaluate first-year students without the student being present. Where do you think this objection comes from?

Protecting Your Marriage From Your Children

Many contemporary parents are so child-centered that their children have little sense that there is a marriage in the house, a marriage that underlies a strong parenting team. Their children never learn to respect the boundaries of their parents' marital relationship. By "boundary," I mean the private zone of a person or a relationship. Many children these days are permitted to interrupt their parents' conversations at any time. If you are married, when was the last time that you asked one of your children to not interrupt a conversation you were having with your spouse? Just as many children have an open door to interrupt their parents' conversations with friends, it's the same for their parents' one-to-one talks with each other.

For many parents, the marital relationship always comes in second to the children's needs and desires. The children have the sense of being at every moment "number one" in the lives of each of their parents, with the needs of the marital relationship quite invisible. Naturally there are many occasions when a child's urgent needs must come first, for example, when a hungry or wet baby needs a quick response. But parents who have difficulty asking children to sacrifice their immediate preferences for the common good of the family won't even think of asking their children to give them a few minutes of private conversation as a couple. The marriage is at the bottom of the priority scale, I believe, in most American families.

When our youngest child was about three, my wife and I created a couple talk ritual after dinner. We would feed the children dessert while we cleaned the dishes and started the coffee. Then we would send the children off to play while we spent about fifteen minutes, over a cup of coffee, catching up with each other. Our expectation was that the children would not bother us during this time unless there was something very important. When they did interrupt us with routine matters, we gently but firmly told them to wait because we were having our coffee talk. Before long, they got the idea and left us in peace for a ritual that became a cornerstone of our marriage.

When Leah and I would talk about this ritual with friends, or I would share it with clients, you would have thought that we were from another planet. Most couples simply cannot imagine their children cooperating with such a ritual. Leaving the parents alone for fifteen minutes? Impossible. Most children won't leave their parents alone for thirty seconds. My response: it's a matter of what we expect and what we are willing to work on with our children. If you start when the children are young, it seems natural to them. Years later, our children would say that it gave them a secure feeling to know that we were communicating with each other. Children's security rests in the quality and endurance of their parents' marriage. They can be taught to respect and support the boundaries of that marriage.

Parents' reluctance to advocate for their own time also shows itself in bedtime routines. It seems that most children nowadays are allowed to stay up until either they choose to go to bed or they fall asleep in front of the television or computer. This makes sense from a child-as-consumer perspective. If you are a customer at a motel, you decide yourself when you are ready for bed. If your son is not sleepy, how do you justify requiring him to go to bed, or to be quiet in his bedroom? Having personal time or couple time is not a good enough reason for many parents to justify—to themselves or to their child—establishing a firm and reasonably early bedtime. The result is that our children are with us, expecting our undivided attention, until they or we collapse for the evening. Trying to change this bedtime-on-demand approach will be met with fierce accusations that you are being arbitrary and unfair—and a poor parental service provider.

My wife and I had firm bedtimes for our children, which we adjusted as they got older. It began with 7:30 for preschool age and went gradually up to 8:30 by the start of junior high. We had a bath and talk ritual that started about thirty minutes before the established bedtime. Our expectation, by the way, was not that the children would go to sleep at the dot of 8:00 p.m., for example, but that they be quietly in bed or in their room. Once they were in elementary school, they were in charge of when they turned the lights. We thus were in control of bedtime, and had time for ourselves as individuals and as a couple, but without trying to control that which parents cannot control—when their children actually go to sleep. If the objective is only that of sleep, when a child claims to not be sleepy at bedtime, then parents feel it is unfair to "make" them go to bed. Our children often stayed up for awhile, reading or playing quietly with a toy, and seemed to enjoy ending the day with some private down time.

When your child becomes a teenager and no longer has a bedtime, you can follow the same principle of asking for respect for your alone time or couple time in the evening. You can ask your teenager to let you know what he or she needs from you earlier in the evening, and then declare yourself at a certain point as "off duty" unless something urgent comes up. Teenagers can learn that, just as they like to be left alone sometimes, their parents do as well. But if you do not calmly assert this boundary in a consistent manner, then your teenagers will be irate that you are not willing to drop everything any time they want your attention.

Supporting Your Co-Parent

In my experience, many two-parent families have just one parent who has high standards for holding the children responsible for good citizenship in the family and community. This parent usually feels unsupported and even undermined by the other parent.

Let's say that Mom is trying to uphold standards of caution and safety with her teenage son's social life. She wants a full description of where he is going on weekend nights, and expects the son to call home if his plans change. Mom wants to know personally the parents of the girl her son is dating. Dad mostly agrees with his wife's concerns, but he is relatively more concerned that her son not be embarrassed among his friends by having parents who are too strict. Dad enjoyed his teenage social life enormously, and wants his own children to be popular and not dragged down by parents. What's more, Dad has convinced himself that the group his son hangs out with are all "good kids." These parents have regular arguments about how closely to monitor and restrict their son.

Can you guess what happens? Over time and many unresolved conflicts, the mother, feeling as if she is the only upholder of standards, comes to act like a suspicious detective, while the father makes excuses for his son and sometimes even lies about how well he knows the family of his son's date. The son then only approaches Dad for permission, and much of the time the mother finds out after the fact. In disgust, she gives up trying.

Or let's say that Dad is the parent who advocates for family dinner rituals. They were important in his growing up years, and he wants the same for his family now. His wife is not against family dinners, but they are not a priority for her—and she's the main cook. As the children get older and push the limits of the dinner ritual—by coming late or scheduling activities during this hour—the father struggles and protests while the mother looks on and makes excuses for them. The children know instinctively when their parents are not together on an expectation. As family dinners erode further, and children want to "graze" before Dad gets home rather than wait to have dinner as a family, the mother starts to graze herself—and then prepares a separate meal for her husband to eat alone when he gets home. She keeps the television news on unless her husband asks her to turn it off. She has joined the children in passive resistance to her husband's "rigid" insistence on family dinners. Eventually, he gives up and becomes a grazer himself.

Sometimes it is important that one parent take a firm stand against the other parent's wishes, especially when those wishes are aimed at pleasing their children's consumer needs. When your spouse is weakening on the matter of your high-school student spending prom night in a hotel, it's time to put your foot down and say no. You can exercise a parental veto, and then later work out your conflict with your spouse. Recently, our local newspapers had a story and photos of young teenage girls at the mall, during a school day, waiting to get autographs from a new teen idol band. Most said that their parents had dropped them off at the mall; one mother even rented a van to bring a group of girls from out of state. Years ago, these kids would have been "playing hooky" from school, without their parents' knowledge, and received detention for this misconduct. Nowadays, their parents freely allow them to skip school because of an exciting opportunity, and then write them a bogus excuse about being sick. The school does its part by looking the other way. In situations where one parent is weakening, I encourage the other parent in the household to say "I will not permit this kind of irresponsible behavior. School comes first! Over my dead body will you go to the mall tomorrow instead of school." I'll bet the child and other parent, although furious, will be secretly relieved that someone in the family is acting like a parent.

But unilateral vetoes cannot be the permanent stuff of parental teamwork. If you want to raise your children as good citizens, spend time and energy getting on the same page with your spouse. Otherwise, you will win some battles but eventually lose the war to the consumer culture of childhood, which is too strong for one parent alone to resist if the other parent is in its embrace. If your spouse will not work with you on these important concerns, then get some help from a marital therapist. The stakes are too high, because the culture is too toxic for children to handle if their parents are divided.

How to Work as a Team Raising Responsible Children

Here are some ideas I've gleaned from my professional and personal experience as a spouse about how to work together with your co-parent:

- Talk openly together about what values you want to promote in your children and how you expect them to behave. Don't assume you both hold the same values or will rank them in the same priority order.

- Clarify your parenting values by discussing specific scenarios in which may come into question: chores, bedtime, meals, church attendance, curfew, dating, disrespectful language.

- Talk specifically about the themes we have discussed in this book. Do you both understand the problem of entitled children taking over their families? What examples have you witnessed? Do you see this as a threat in your own family?

- Examine your differences and speak of them openly. Does one of you tend to be "softer" with the children and the other "harder"? Try to surface these differences without making one of you the bad parent.

- Agree that you will try to work with, and some times blend, your parenting differences, and that you will both support the final decision.

- When you have agreed on major expectations for your children, you should both take responsibility for enforcing them. If dinner is to be sharply at six o'clock, both parents should enforce the rule, even if one of them feels more strongly about it.

- Be alert to how your children are treating your spouse. Do not tolerate disrespect to either of you.

- If you find yourselves getting locked into "enforcer" versus "easy going" roles with the children, deliberately plan a period of time to reverse these roles, or reverse them around certain agreed-upon issues. For example, let the easygoing parent take over enforcing the chores or getting the children ready for bed.

- If you have concerns about your partner's parenting behavior, talk about it in private rather than undermining the partner in front of the children.

- Make sure that all major policies and decisions are thoroughly aired between the two of you, before being shared with the children.

- Work diligently to carve out time and space for your own relationship. Ideally, this includes some time each day to talk as a couple and a date outside of the home at least every other week.

Children cling not only to their parents, but to their parents' relationship with each other. Loving, cooperative two-parent families are clearly the best environment for today's children to be raised in. But having two parents in the home does not automatically guarantee the children will be good citizens. If the parents are divided, the results could be disastrous. That's why I say that two-parent families are the best and the worst places for raising children. May yours be the best.

CONFIDENT FATHERING

I want to spend a chapter on fatherhood because fathers are often left out of discussions of effective parenting. In fact, when people refer to generic "parenting," they are usually talking about what mothers do.

In past times, fathers were considered the chief parent in charge of children's moral development. In the seventeenth and eighteenth centuries, fathers were expected to read the Bible to the children and assure their children's proper behavior. Mothers at this time were considered too emotional and unsteady to be in charge of such an important part of child rearing. One historian characterized this traditional role of fathers as the "moral overseer."

This role changed drastically in the nineteenth century when fathers moved into the industrial labor force and families migrated to the cities. Mothers at that time were expected to provide a "haven in a heartless world," a place of emotional security and character development in a strange, urban environment. Whereas earlier fathers were present to their children as co-workers during the day in farming communities, when fathers took jobs in factories they were gone from the family living area for most of the day. Although tradition still referred to them as the "head" of the family, in fact their role diminished in the home to that of back up for the mother, and sometimes-stern disciplinarian of last resort. Outside the home, of course, fathers were seen as the sole wage earner, a role that was theirs almost exclusively until the latter part of the twentieth century.

For about one hundred years there have been a number of social movements attempting to make fathers less aloof and more nurturing with their children. My colleague Ralph La Rossa has shown how the term "dad" arose in the early twentieth century as a way to suggest that fathers could be "buddies" and playmates with children, not stern task masters. It appears now that "dad" has replaced "father" in the lexicon of parenting, and that the father's special role in two-parent families is that of playing with his children—especially his young children—plus being "back up" for Mom. Mothers are still defined as the primary parent, but one who also works outside of the home and earns money. In fact, the role of mothers has changed more than the role of fathers.

Do you see a problem with defining fathers as playmates and backups? I certainly do. Too often, fathers are not expected to do the hard work of raising responsible children—the down and dirty work of making sure they do their chores and homework, of making sure they show respect for others, of organizing family rituals, of creating opportunities for children to contribute to their community. Raising citizens occurs mostly in the trenches of family life, where mothers tend to dwell and fathers tend to only visit.

The Father as Brute

In addition to Dad as nice guy, we have another, strikingly different image of the father in contemporary society: the father as angry, hurtful, and abusive. Fathers in the middle ground are harder to name these days.

I was stunned by what two different colleagues told me. Each recounted the stories of male relatives on public outings with their toddlers who began to act up. In one case the child ran away and the father gave chase to retrieve him. In the other case the child started screaming in the supermarket, whereupon the father picked him up. Both fathers were confronted suspiciously by strangers, both women, about whether in fact these men were the child's father. Feeling humiliated, both offered stumbling reassurances that they were indeed the father and not a kidnapper.

I cannot imagine a mother being confronted in the same way for physically restraining her toddler in public. We have discovered the dark, abusive side of men in our culture. A male student of mine once volunteered to do childcare for a women's march against violence. He noticed that some of the children wore tags that said, "Not to be touched by a man." While he was pushing a young child on a swing, the child on the next swing suddenly fell to the ground. My student rushed to her side, but was quickly intercepted by a female childcare volunteer who screamed, "Not to be touched by a man! Not to be touched by a man!" The child indeed was wearing that tag, which my student had failed to notice in his urgency about helping. Like the fathers confronted in public, he felt humiliated—as if he were unclean. What are we saying to our children about men?

Although most mothers do not consider their children's father an abuser, I have noticed that the therapeutic culture of parenting sometimes puts mothers in the position of being a protector of the children from the father's anger and a critic of the way he expresses his frustration with the children. In one common scenario, the mother believes that raising one's voice is a frightening experience for young children. As a good therapeutic parent, she herself tries to refrain from yelling. But her husband, less trained in modern, sensitive parenting practices, allows himself to yell at their child when he is upset. I am not talking about screaming, just raising his voice.

The mother is convinced that her husband's yelling is harmful to the child. As evidence, she points to the fact that the child sometimes cries when the father raises his voice—whereupon the mother rushes to the child's side to offer consolation. Can you see what a set up this is for the child to manipulate? Of course it's not fun to have a parent yell at you, and sometimes it's downright upsetting. But if a child can get the attention away from misdeeds and onto hurt feelings, he or she can emerge victorious.

Outside of the child's presence, the mother confronts the father about his temper. She tells him he is too big and too loud for this child. She says she herself sometimes feels intimidated by his anger, and she can only imagine how frightening it is to a young child. Most fathers are no match for this kind of challenge, partly because few men have an explicit philosophy of child rearing and therefore most lack confidence in how they are handling themselves. If the mother quotes child-rearing authorities or uses therapeutic language, the father cannot counter with anything other than his intuitions, which are not, in this culture, supposed to be as good as a mother's.

Notice too how the mother in this example brings in the marital issues, as if she and her child are standing against the brutish husband and father. Most fathers will either back off disciplining their child or will stubbornly continue their current practices. Either way everyone loses: if the father backs off, he is less of a parent, and if he stubbornly continues, the mother will keep on rescuing the child and criticizing the father. The child will understand the dynamic pretty quickly. The mother, too, will be undermined in this situation.

When I meet with families like this one, I first observe the child's relationship with the father. I try to evaluate the quality of the father-child bond and the actual level of nastiness or intimidation in the father's behavior. In many cases, my assessment is that the mother has embraced an unrealistic therapeutic approach to parenting—an anger-phobic approach—and that her own problems with her husband are spilling over to parenting. Most often I see a child who is thoroughly bonded to the father, who feels loved by him, and who can easily survive an episode of Dad's anger. As for the child's occasional tearful reactions, some young children respond that way to parental anger, just as others get stubborn. Most often the child ceases the negative behavior that the father was challenging, and a few minutes later is willing to crawl into his arms to play or fall asleep. The only damage results from the mother's hypersensitive reaction. You can convince children that they have been wounded if you over-respond to their distress.

I do not mean to suggest that the fathers in these scenarios have nothing to learn. Many times the father is yelling in a non-productive way because he does not know what else to do with a disobedient child. The problem is not that he is hurting his child, it's that he is being ineffective if he is yelling too much. Parents who yell the most are usually the most ineffective because their children tune them out. But taking his behavior out of the domain of abuse frees him up to learn a wider repertoire of responses to his child, and for the mother to expand her repertoire of parenting skills as well.

Being Firm

As I mentioned before, most fathers nowadays seem to err on the side of being too nice when it comes to shaping their children as citizens of the family and community. Many of these men are trying to be different from their own fathers, whom they felt were emotionally distant and too stern. Contemporary young fathers want very much to be close to their children. This section is about fathers who live with their children full time. In a later section, I will address fathers who do not live with their children full time.

It's wonderful that so many fathers want to be close to their children. The problem is that being close sometimes involves being the one to stay with a decision that is good for the family but unpopular with one of the children. Many times fathers don't feel that they have enough equity in their relationship with their children to withstand their children's anger and disappointment when this occurs.

Contrary to some popular stereotypes, men tend to be conflict evaders, not conflict starters. Research shows that women bring up most conflict issues in marriage, and that mothers are more apt to challenge their children's behavior. Men prefer to keep the peace in their close relationships, even if this means not dealing with difficulties. This difference can create problems in co-parenting when children learn to expect Dad to cease all disciplinary conflict when it gets uncomfortable for him.

Take the example of Paul and his family. When Paul is home from his stressful job in the factory, he wants to have a peaceful home life. He does have his own moments of irritability, mostly when he wants his children to leave him alone. But he is not an active confronter of the children. When his wife Mary is locked into a battle with their fourteen-year-old daughter about doing her chores or where she is going for the evening, Paul gets frustrated by all the loud and angry commotion. He sometimes tells both his wife and his daughter to settle down, thereby completely undermining his wife. When she turns her anger on him, he grows sullen and criticizes her for her negative attitude. Meanwhile, the daughter is off the hook. She has learned that if she makes a big enough fuss with Mom, Dad will bail her out. It is hard to raise a responsible child in these circumstances.

How can these fathers learn to be firm? I believe it's mostly about being an involved, hands-on parent. It's easy to be a conflict-avoiding nice guy if you are not on duty that much. Fathers, you see, tend to parent mostly in the presence of the mother, usually in a triangle with the mother and the child. Mothers, on the other hand, tend to have much more solo time with their children. This means that mothers are forced to develop their skills not only in nurturing and comforting children, but also in disciplining them and enforcing expectations of them. Fathers, who for whatever reason are not alone with their children as often, have a more difficult time developing certain parenting skills.

When fathers let their wives be the point person for the most intense times in raising children—comforting a troubled or hurt child, and disciplining an irresponsible child—they cheat themselves out of the deepest experiences of being a parent. Being deeply involved is the ultimate solution to the problem of the nice guy father. Later in this chapter I will give specific advice about how to pull this off.

Father as Consultant on Morals and Social Behavior

A traditional positive role of fathers was to be a moral guide and an adviser about finding one's way in the larger world community. It still is today, though mothers also play this role well. In teaching social values to their children, many fathers (and some mothers) make the mistake of talking too much and listening too little. The old idea of *paterfamilias* holding forth on the state of the world does not work anymore, if it ever did. The most effective way for parents to communicate values is to first listen and explore the child's feelings and beliefs, and then tailor their own words carefully.

Let's say that you overhear your twelve-year-old son making fun of another boy in school for being a "fag." Here you have an opportunity to try to influence your son's attitudes towards kids who are seen as different or unpopular. An ineffective approach would be to give a speech about acceptance and tolerance. Your son will click off and probably just go underground with his attitudes if you do this.

A better approach would be, at a quiet moment, to ask your son about the boy you heard him speaking of earlier. How does he know the boy? What is the boy like? Do the other kids make fun of this boy? Why? Does your son know what the word "fag" means? Why is he using that word? How does the boy react when people make fun of him? How do you think he feels? You should not ask these questions in rapid-fire fashion. Rather you should let the conversation unfold depending on the openness of your son. Your approach should center on understanding where your son is coming from with his remarks, what values and attitudes he has picked up, and why he is acting towards the other boy the way he is.

If this exploration goes well, you are in a position to let your son know your own values. Rather than doing this didactically, however, it is often best to fold your values into the discussion. In the scenario we are discussing, I might first let my son know that I appreciate how confusing it can be for him to sort out how he feels about this other boy. I would also stress how difficult life must be for this other boy who is being mocked by the other kids. It's hard to be different at that age. I might say that it's cruel for kids to isolate and make fun of others for being different.

On the subject of homosexuality, depending on my son's openness in the conversation, I might say that being gay or straight seems to be something people are born with, and that I think it is unfair when people act hatefully towards someone for something they cannot control. Of course, having this kind of open conversation would require that we had already had a number of conversations about sexuality.

You might approach this last part of the discussion differently, depending on your values about homosexuality, but my general point is that being a consultant about our children's social values involves lots of listening, a few carefully-selected statements of your own beliefs and perspectives, and letting the conversation end. Your child can then think about what has been said.

Other opportunities to influence social values can be taken from the news. While I was writing this book, President Clinton's impeachment trial was taking place. Some parents took the opportunity to explore with their children the values of honesty and fidelity. They discussed how a person could be good at many aspects of his or her work but still act irresponsibly in private matters. Openly discussing what children cannot avoid seeing in the media provides a vehicle for values education. But remember to begin with your child's own knowledge and opinions.

Discussing public policy issues gives you opportunities, especially with teenagers, to explore social values. In the case of welfare, for example, a discussion could center on the value of self-initiative for individuals versus the value of society's responsibility to care for the needy. As my children grew more aware of the world, I looked for opportunities to bring up issues of social importance, often at the dinner table or when the family was out for our weekly trip to the pizza parlor. It's important not to force these conversations, however, or they will be counter-productive.

A benefit of genuine dialogue about social values is that our children will also teach us. I remember clearly the time that I said something dismissive about a political party, along the lines of "They don't care a bit about poor people." My sixteen-year-old son challenged me about this generalized putdown, and I took it to heart. After that exchange, I have made a point to speak in a more specific way about the positions of the political parties and candidates, rather than indulging in broad-brush attacks.

Our children can also teach us tolerance of parts of the youth culture that we do not understand, such as certain kinds of music and fads. If we are willing to listen, our children can help us get past the surface to see what some of these things mean to young people. I remember my daughter pointing out qualities she admired in singer/actress Madonna: how she ran her own career and changed her appearance often rather than being stuck in one media image. I subsequently went with her to see one of Madonna's movies, and we had a good discussion afterwards. I was still troubled with certain values Madonna was portraying, and told my daughter so. But I could then see what my daughter appreciated about Madonna. If we are open to our children's values and experiences, they are more open to ours.

How to Be an Influential Father

As I have stressed, the tendency of fathering today is to be a nice guy and an assistant to the mother. Yet it is worth the effort for fathers to become more involved and connected, and have more influence in their children's lives. Here are some ideas for how to do this:

- Spend as much solo time with your children as possible, starting from the time they are born. There is no substitute for being the sole person in charge of a child's care. Being alone with your child not only helps you to develop a more special bond with your child, it also encourages your own spontaneity and problem-solving skills.

- See yourself as "on duty" for parenting whenever you are home, unless you and your spouse have negotiated down time. Don't assume you can tune out the children because your wife is around.

- Avoid "handing over" a child to his or her mother when you get frustrated. You don't hand over the wheel of the car when traffic is frustrating.

- Resist the attempts of your wife to rescue you when you are in charge of the children. If you are feeding the baby, hang in there when the child gets fussy and don't let your wife automatically take over—unless there are also times when you take over from her.

- Children who are accustomed to their mother's involvement at special times like bedtime rituals will sometimes resist the father's involvement. Resist your child's attempts to decide that Mom will be permanently in charge of important activities like this. Don't let your child vote you out of parenting. Your children are not the store customers who can decide which clerk to ask for help.

- Support your wife with the children. This means backing up her discipline, giving her a respite, and offering her moral support.

- Do at least half of the limit setting with the children. This will not compromise your positive relationship with the children, and it will make you a better parent and partner.

- Read books about parenting and family life and share these ideas with your wife. Don't just rely on your wife to research and develop a philosophy of how to raise children.

- Take more leadership in family rituals such as meals. Be active in putting on a ritual that you are solely responsible for.

- Develop a wide repertoire of parenting skills— from playing, to nurturing, to listening, to limit setting—and practice them all.

- Look for opportunities to respectfully share your values with your children.

- Work on maintaining your marriage, and protect it from the children.

Fathering is perhaps the greatest under-tapped resource we have for raising responsible children. Many fathers are operating at about one-third capacity, mostly because of cultural expectations. Children become the best citizens of families and communities when they have a hands-on father who can do *all* the jobs of being a parent.

Confident Single Parenting

Other than attempting to parent in a severely conflicted two-parent family, single parenting is the most difficult form of parenting. A single parent must have unusually good parenting instincts, and lots of courage, to be able to raise children to be good citizens. This chapter looks at the two faces of single parenting—the experience of the main custodial parent (usually the mother) and the experience of the non-custodial parent (usually the father).

First, some history and some facts: About one-third of all children now live in a single-parent family. Single-parent families experience poverty rates far higher than two-parent families. Until the late twentieth century most people became a single parent through the death of their spouse. Nowadays the most common paths to single parenting are through divorce and through bearing a child outside of marriage.

Research shows that single parents have more difficulty with monitoring their children's behavior—knowing where they are and what they are up to. And they have more difficulty with setting limits, tending to be too permissive and then exploding with ineffective anger. It's not a completely bleak picture, however. Many single parents are quite successful in raising children, and, despite the challenges, most children in single-parent families do grow up to be productive adults.

The next section maps out the special challenges of single parents along with some ways to master these challenges.

Single Mothers Who Raise Children Alone

The hour before dinner is one of the most draining hours in any family. This hour is twice as hectic in single-parent families. Mom comes home from work tired and already emotionally fried, having run errands and nearly missed her car pool assignment to drive four children to soccer practice. The children are hungry for both food and Mom's attention. They are on each other's nerves. There is nothing good on television, and Mom won't let anyone snack before dinner.

Charging into the kitchen, Mom greets her twelve-year-old daughter Kristen, who immediately asks to go to a boy-girl sleepover the coming Friday night.

Mom responds angrily, "You are not going to a boy-girl sleepover at your age."

Kristen mumbles loud enough for Mom to hear, "Oh, go to hell."

"Don't you talk to me that way," Mom retorts.

"Why not?" replies Kristen. "You've talked that way to me before."

The conflict escalates further. Mom tells Kristen she will have no special privileges because she has not done her basic chores.

Kristen explodes: "I hate your f___ guts."

Losing it, Mom pushes Kristen out of the room, screaming at her to "get out of my sight and forget about having any privileges until you are eighteen."

Dinner, anyone?

I have seen lots of single-parent families with scenes like this one, with children showing verbal disrespect for their harried mother who at first takes too much and then, finally, loses her cool. These families do not have these scenes right away, however. They start with smaller incidents. Kristen's mother had been giving in to her for years, always acquiescing to her demands, which typically included demands for the latest consumer product marketed toward kids.

Such scenes occur in two-parent families too. But single parents are particularly at risk for giving in to their children's persistent demands and later, when the demands become too great or unreasonable (like going to a boy-girl sleepover), the frazzled mother and spoiled child reach the point like Kristen and her mother did.

Without another adult around for moral support, it is more difficult for single parents to displease their children because they also rely on their children for support. Additionally, when there are two or more children, the kids outnumber the parent, further harrying her and leading to the potential for an emotional outburst.

Thus single mothers have difficulty maintaining high standards for their children's conduct. A peer, sibling-like tone creeps into the relationship. Some of this is for the good, as children learn to contribute to family chores and to understand that parents have good days and bad days. But sometimes the peer flavor goes too far, and mom loses her authority. You can't go from buddy to authority figure very easily without your children feeling angry and betrayed.

I used the word "betrayed" deliberately because children will feel that their mother has turned on them when she pulls rank. As Kristen once objected to her mother, "But I thought we were friends." Mom retorted, "I'm not your friend. I'm your mother." But they both knew that a lot of evidence pointed the other direction—that mom had treated her daughter like a peer. Imagine someone who was your friend or sister suddenly trying to be your boss. No way would you accept this without a fight.

Being a peer to one's children does not translate to getting along well with them. Usually it means the opposite. It means that in arguments it's hard to determine who is taking the role of the parent and who is taking the role of the child. The kid screams insults and the parent screams insults back. The parent gets sarcastic and so does the kid. The kid curses and the parent curses. Sometimes the kid gives in to the parent in order to keep the peace, and other times the parent gives in for the same reason. Here's an example of how this kind of dialogue goes:

Mom: Kristen, you have to clean your room today.
Kristen: I already cleaned it.
Mom: Not to my satisfaction.
Kristen: Who cares about your satisfaction? It's my room.
Mom: It's a pigsty.
Kristen: Yeah, like your room isn't a pigsty?
Mom: My room is my business.
Kristen: So is my room.
Mom: If you don't clean your room today, you are grounded.
Kristen: Fine.

Do you see the pivotal point at which mom allowed Kristen to talk to her like a peer or roommate? It was the point when the girl's language became disrespectful. It's easy to miss if you stay focused, as this mother did, on the topic of the room. The first point of disrespect came with the line "Who cares about your satisfaction?" Note that this would be a perfectly acceptable thing to say to a sibling who was complaining about his sister's room. When said to a parent, it is a direct challenge to the legitimacy of the parent's authority. It erases the boundaries between the parent and child.

Unfortunately Mom did not know how to respond directly to the challenge to her authority. So she escalated her language by characterizing her daughter's room as a "pigsty." As parents, we know instinctively when our children cross the line into disrespectful challenge to our authority. If we don't do something directly about it, right away, we will take it out on them in some other way. In this case, mom resorted to inflammatory language.

The second point of disrespect and direct invasion of the parent's boundary was when Kristen said that Mom's room was a pigsty too. Mom tried to regain her parental status by claiming that her room was her own business, not her daughter's. But by that point Kristen was well into the challenge to her mother's authority, and asserted that her room was her own business as well, and not her mother's. Does this sound like two sisters, or quarreling roommates? Mom then tried to pull rank by threatening to ground Kristen, who at that point is disgusted with the conversation. They both know that Mom will not follow through on the grounding because she cannot tolerate another meltdown argument when Kristen decides to go out that night.

It's harder to handle being unpopular with your children when you are the only adult in the home. If you have another parent who is reasonably supportive, you can lick your wounds and feel reassured that you did the right thing in asserting your expectations of your children. Even if you messed up, you have someone to process it with. If your children are angry with you, you can talk to your spouse. If another confrontation is brewing, you can ask your spouse to handle it. It's difficult when you are the only adult on duty.

Complicating the challenge of raising responsible children in single-parent families is the relationship between the mother and father—how they broke up, and how they currently get along. Children sometimes feel angry and let down that their parents did not stay together and provide a two-parent home. They sometimes feel resentful, especially towards the parent they believe was primarily responsible for breaking up the family. They view their parents' dating of other people, and possibly remarriage, as further betrayals. These strong feelings easily can come out in a sense of entitlement—you owe me a lot after what you did to me—and rebellion against the single parent's authority.

Children who feel let down by their parents will have more trouble respecting them, at least for a time. They will challenge parents' right to discipline them. But for our children's own good as well as our own, we have to insist on respect and cooperation. The traffic accident that injured your child may have been your fault, but you still have to make sure your child goes to the doctor (even if he or she does not want to) and works on recovering at home. We all unintentionally hurt our children, but that does not mean we permit open season on parent bashing.

Research consistently has shown that the major negative factor for children in divorce is ongoing conflict between the parents. It pulls children in two directions, creating bad feelings about both parents. When Dad is late picking up the children, Mom says, "He is never reliable." When the children tell Dad they wish they saw him more often, he puts it all on the other parent with the words, "I would love to, but your mother won't let me." Children caught in this crossfire will resent both parents, withdraw their willingness to cooperate, feel entitled to get what they want, and engage in angry, disrespectful outbursts.

This is another chance for me to say something I regard as very important to my message. When our children's behavior problems or disrespectful language stem directly from our failings as parents, we have to work to eliminate those failings or at least reduce their damage. If your marriage is already over, you can't readily resurrect it for your children's sake. But you can conscientiously refrain from criticizing your ex-spouse in front of your children. You can redouble your efforts to cooperate with your ex, and to not use the children as intermediaries. If immediately following the divorce you were distracted and inattentive towards your children, then it won't be enough to challenge their negative behavior. You've got to spend more time with them and get back in touch with them again.

Although I have been emphasizing how parents must take back their authority with their children, it's ultimately the children who give us permission to exercise our authority, based on their sense that we love them, care for them, and treat them fairly. Children who feel unprotected and treated unfairly, as they do when their parents are at war, will withdraw their willingness to work with us. If our children do not sense our unbreakable commitment to their welfare, no amount of effective disciplinary skills will work. We won't get them back unless we change our hearts and fix our own behavior. The majority of good parenting involves working on ourselves, not our kids.

Guidelines and Strategies for Single Parents

The guidelines and strategies previously covered for all parents certainly apply to those who are single parents. The focus in this section is on strategies that have special relevance to full time single parents (women and men) who are trying to confidently raise responsible children:

- Remember: you are the parent. Do not argue with your children as if you were their sister or brother.

- Minimize the amount of debating you do with your children. Instead, after you've talked and listened enough, say, "This discussion is over."

- Avoid, as much as possible, caving in after a long period of whining from your children. We used to tell our daughter that whining meant an automatic "no."

- Buy time for decisions by saying, "I'll think about it and get back to you." Some cave-ins occur because you decide too quickly to say "no," and upon reflection, you realize you were wrong.

- Talk to a trusted friend or relative about issues of parenting, particularly the major policy decisions. We all need to bounce our feelings and thoughts off someone who knows and loves us and our children.

- Be willing to listen to your children's feelings about your divorce or break up. Ask them to share their feelings about what it's like to be in a divided family, about your dating situation, and their thoughts on possible remarriage. If your children can express their hurt, fear, or anger directly in calm, open moments, they are less apt to act out these feelings by defying your authority.

- Insist that your children speak to you with respect at all times. Allow no disrespect to go unchallenged, or eventually they will show little respect at all.

- Expect as much respect and cooperation from your sons as you do from your daughters. Note to mothers: even if your son is bigger than you are, remember that parental authority does not depend on physical strength. My mother was a foot shorter than me when I was in high school, but her authority never wavered.

- Work hard on cooperating with your children's other parent. Never let a negative word come from your mouth about him or her, although you don't have to deny your children's feelings if they complain about the other parent. Never ask the children to be message bearers.

- Maintain your family rituals around such things as mealtimes, bedtimes, and special outings. Although your children might resist, keep in mind that family rituals are a big part of the glue that holds your family together after a break up. Even if you cannot do family dinners every night, make them special when you do have them.

- Work hard at preparing for the transition times that are so difficult in single-parent families—for example, the times of shifting between house holds. Talk with your children and your ex about how to make these transitions go more smoothly.

- Have regular family meetings with your children to calmly discuss their behavior and their family citizenship. You will be much more effective if you bring things up at scheduled moments than when you are emotionally and physically drained and your children are also out of sorts.

Advice for Single Fathers

This section addresses single fathers who do not live with their children full time or even half time. These fathers come to single parenting with a series of challenges. They probably did not do much one-on-one parenting when they were married to the mother. They probably hurt and disappointed their children when they left the home. And they have such a limited schedule with their children that it is hard to function as a well-rounded parent.

In general, if the custodial parent's burden is too much solo time with the children, the non-custodial parent's burden is too little time.

The first rule for non-custodial fathers (and mothers) is that they be faithful to being with their children at the agreed upon times. Inconsistency makes the father untrustworthy in the eyes of his children. Even if you do not have enough time with your children, you owe them your unflagging commitment to the time you do have with them. Without that commitment, you can forget about helping them be good citizens of their family and community—because you are not being a good citizen yourself.

When you are with your children, resist the temptation to act like a recreation director. Do fun things, but have a real life with them as well: run errands, cook meals, watch some television. Let them hang out some of the time, playing with their own toys, or watching their favorite video.

Expect your children to be contributors to your family life with them, not just consumers. They should help with cleaning up, especially the spaces they occupy. They should be expected to not interrupt you when you are on the phone. They should be expected to do family obligations such as visiting your relatives. I am not suggesting that you fail to plan an enjoyable weekend, but that in the midst of the enjoyment you treat your children naturally, as having both needs and responsibilities.

Charging around from one event to another wears thin on both the single father and his children. Children get tired, physically and emotionally, from too much stimulation. They will complain that they are bored when not hyper-stimulated, but they will become exhausted from too much busyness.

Too little time together makes some single fathers reluctant to "spoil" the time by being a disciplinarian. In the short term you can buy the children's cooperation by giving in to their demands. This only works for a while. Ask them too often to decide what's for dinner and they will refuse to eat what you select on your own.

If single mothers sometimes manipulate their ex-spouse by messing with the visitation schedule, single fathers sometimes manipulate by withholding child support payments. Both of these activities undermine the sense of justice that must underlie family life. Even if the children do not know the details, they will sense that their parents are letting them down. As a non-custodial parent, you will have no moral leverage with your children or your ex-spouse unless you faithfully pay your child support—no matter how uncooperative your ex is about visitation and no matter how poorly she spends the money. The deal is that we each have to do the right thing by our children, not matter what our ex-spouse is doing.

Most of all, see your relationship with your children as solid and forever, not fragile and temporary. That means not just seeking to please them, but also being able to make demands on them. As they get older and have more complex schedules, you will insist that you see them at least as often as before. Some single fathers let their children drift away when they get over-involved in sports and other scheduled activities. Do not move to an on-demand schedule with your teenagers in which you see them at their convenience. You will become marginal in their lives. This will satisfy their immediate desires for maximum freedom of schedule, but they will end up resenting you and distancing themselves from you as they enter adulthood. No child should be free to choose not to spend time with a parent, unless that parent is abusive or dangerous. Parents are not providers whose services are no longer required.

Single parents can easily see themselves as catering to children as if they are demanding consumers. The alternative path is to expect as much of your children as you do of yourself—that they be contributors to your family life as well as receivers, that they be as faithful to being your child as you are to being their parent.

CONFIDENT PARENTING IN STEPFAMILIES

Even experienced, confident parents lose their footing when they enter a stepfamily. Every stepfamily begins with a love affair that represents the renewal of hope for the man and woman, but then most often enters an extended period of confusion and distress. "Step" is from the Old English word for "bereaved." Stepfamilies, you see, are born in loss as well as in love. For reasons I will discuss, this may be the hardest type of family in which to confidently raise children as responsible citizens of both their families and communities. Stepfamilies succeed only when the adults have grit, courage, commitment, and flexibility.

Stepfamilies have been around forever, but until recently most were formed after the death of a parent. There is a long cultural legacy of negativity towards stepparents, especially "wicked" stepmothers. Nowadays about half of all new marriages are remarriages for one or both partners following a divorce, and most of these marriages involve children. Research on stepfamilies shows that they are at greater risk for violence and abuse than original families. Second marriages are also more likely to end in divorce. Despite the presence of two adults and the additional household income, stepfamilies do not drastically raise the income level from above the average for single-parent families.

In fact, with stepfamilies come new stresses. In stepfamilies, as nowhere else, adults are often out of step with everything our children want. Adults want to remarry and the kids want them to stay single—or remarry their original spouse.

Adults want to move to a new house not previously owned by either mate, and the children want to keep their old house, neighborhood, and school. Adults want to re-create an original, tightly bonded family, and the kids yearn for the days when they had their parent to themselves. Adults want the children to bond immediately with their new stepparent, and they feel disloyal to their other parent if they do.

There is little doubt that in stepfamilies adults occupy different emotional worlds than children. More than in any other family form, children do not "sign up" as citizens of new stepfamilies, at least not for several years. Many of them remain "conscientious objectors" to a regime they did not welcome. Sometimes they are more belligerent objectors.

If the internal dynamics of stepfamilies are formidable, consider the external dynamics. There are many external saboteurs. There are ex-spouses who convince themselves that this remarriage is a personal affront and a threat to their children's well being. This is especially true with aggrieved ex-spouses who felt dumped and who have not remarried themselves. An antagonistic ex-spouse can single-handedly make life hell for a stepfamily, driving wedges between generations and between spouses.

Then there are two or three families of origin—yours, who never wanted you to get divorced in the first place; your ex's, who blame you for abandoning their son or daughter; and your new spouse's family, who think you have too much baggage to be a good mate. The half of your couple friends that you kept after the divorce may be cut in half again when asked to befriend your new spouse.

Opposition is not limited to those closest to you. For added measure, throw in the passive undermining of teachers, coaches, and doctors who pretend the stepparent does not exist and won't deal at all with the non-custodial parent. And when stepfamilies come to therapy, therapists are often not much help, and sometimes make things worse, because they don't understand their unique and complex dynamics.

I have laid out the challenges so starkly in order to make the point that it takes considerable work and patience to build an enduring stepfamily that is a healthy place for raising children. The first mistake that remarried couples make is to assume that a stepfamily is just like an original family. The second mistake is to assume that the adjustment period will be smooth and brief. The keys to successful stepfamily life comes from understanding that stepfamilies are different and that the adjustment takes a number of years, not weeks or months.

The Importance of Loyalty in Stepfamilies

If you grew up with your biological parents, you probably assumed that your survival and well-being were central to their own happiness, and that they would die for you if necessary. Even if your parents were mean at times, or too controlling, you probably knew that you were the top priority in their lives. Unless your family was terribly disabled, you could count on your parents' fundamental loyalty—and they on yours. Loyalty, the preferential commitment to someone, is the linchpin of family life. Loyalty is a quality that is taken for granted in original families. Loyalty cannot be taken for granted in stepfamilies.

In stepfamilies, loyalty is much more complex. Children who genuinely like their stepparents often refrain from seeming too loyal to them out of fear of betraying their original parent of the same sex. I will tell you a story that makes this point in a touching way:

In a near whisper, six-year-old Rachel told me that she did something she felt bad about after each visit to the two stepfamilies she shuttled between. Rachel had written down these feelings and experiences in a notebook so she would not forget them in the annual "check up" session that she, her brother, and her divorced parents had with me. When I asked what she did that made her feel bad, she said that she always said something a little mean about what happened in the other family, often something the stepparent did or said. Sometimes, she confessed, she made those things up.

Rachel told me that when she did this she felt guilty because she genuinely liked both of the stepparents, as well as her original parents. She didn't think either family was

127

hoping to hear these criticisms, and certainly no one was asking for them. These small loyalty violations, and the attendant guilt, were coming from her six-year-old heart. After talking with her for a while, I asked if she was okay with telling her parents about her feelings. She was willing but asked me to go first in explaining things to them. The parents responded with empathy and reassurance after I brought them back into the room, and Rachel subsequently broke her cycle of small betrayals and guilt.

Another misdirected case of child loyalty was less gratifying, at least at first, because the situation was caused by the parent:

Roy was still smarting from the divorce his wife had insisted on. He enjoyed seeing his two boys, ages seven and five, during visitations, while he tried to piece his life back together. During his first therapy session, he told me how afraid he was of losing his sons, now that there was a new father figure living with them. I tried to be reassuring about his irreplaceable role in their lives, especially if he maintained steady connection with them.

In the second session, Roy told me that one of his boys had slipped and referred to their stepfather as "Dad." Roy summarily told both children that if they started calling their stepfather "Dad," he would never see them again. Roy came across as proud of how he had stood up for his rights. I was horrified at this profound threat to these young children: lose your father if you let him know you are close to your stepfather. I saw this as a family emergency because his sons were living with these feelings at the very moment I was talking with Roy.

As much as I felt like saying, "What in the hell are you doing to your children?" I started low key, with empathy for his fear and pain, and then asked questions about how he thought his children felt about what he told them. Roy was a loving father, and he immediately began to see, with a little prompting from me, what he had done. My goal then was to enhance his sense of urgency to makes things right with the children. I told him that I thought this was an emergency in his relationship with his sons, one that I urged him to attend to right away—that evening if possible—because they were living with the terrible fear that they had alienated him forever.

With tears, Roy told me that there was nothing they could ever do to make him leave them. I urged him to say that to his children, to apologize to them, and to bring them to a therapy session next week to continue to work on restoring trust. This experience was a moral crucible for Roy, an experience that propelled him out of his self-pity after the divorce and re-solidified his commitment to his children. We cannot expect loyalty and responsible behavior from our children unless they feel our unbreakable commitment to them. New stepfamilies sometimes create shock waves that threaten this loyal commitment.

Stepfamilies and the Consumer Culture of Childhood

It isn't only the children in stepfamilies who have questions of loyalty. Original parents and stepparents do as well, but it's difficult to manage adult needs when children are the sole center of the family universe. Rob wanted some time alone with his new wife, Alice, who had three preteen children who took up most of her time. He was good with the children, and supportive of Alice, but felt like a junior parent and not a spouse. Their therapist told me about the session where this issue came to a head. The therapist supported the wife's obligations to her children and encouraged the husband to understand that she needed his support as a very busy mother who also had an outside job. As an adult, his needs would have to be secondary at this time in the family's life cycle, as is true, the therapist noted, for most families in the busy child-rearing years.

The therapist felt proud of his intervention, especially after Alice wept with the sense of being understood and Rob admitted that perhaps he was being selfish. But the therapy was stalled, and the gulf between Alice and Rob widened.

What the therapist had missed, in focusing on the mother's sense of obligation to her children, was the husband's loyalty claims on his wife that went beyond their parent-stepparent roles. Bob was asking for time to be like married partners and not just co-parents. His wife was responding with the defense that nothing different was possible because the children's needs had to come first. What wasn't pointed out to them was that the "children first" mantra is only a starting point for exploring family responsibilities, not an end point or a conversation stopper.

Marital bonds bring their own obligations to love, cherish, and spend time together as partners. And respect for these obligations is particularly important in stepfamilies, where the new spouse does not have the same investment in the children. New spouses choose their married partner, and the children "come with." It is not reasonable to expect them to put the marriage on hold for years until the children grow up. Nurturing a marriage and caring for children are not mutually exclusive activities.

This is where the consumer culture of childhood affects stepfamilies. If original parents see themselves as providers of services to demanding children, the new spouse will feel left out and resentful. And it isn't just mothers who get into being parent providers. Along with other therapists, I am beginning to see a new phenomenon with remarried fathers: when they have their children on the custody schedule, they are totally focused on their children, to the exclusion of their wives.

Often feeling guilty about the divorce, these men are determined to stay close to their children. Their new wives have mixed feelings. On the one hand, the new wife admires her husband for his commitment to his children. On the other hand, she thinks that his loyalties are over-balanced towards his children.

The husband responds to his wife's complaints by saying that he does not have his children full time anymore, and wants to use the limited time well. He explains that he focuses on her the rest of the time when they are not around. She replies that she dreads the days his children are around, even though she genuinely likes the kids, because she feels like she does not have a husband. She adds that he uses the time when the children are not around to do all the tasks he postpones when they are there. So it's not like she gets his full attention when his children are not with them.

When I inquire about what the father is doing with his children in these situations, I often see the earmarks of the consumer culture of childhood. His kids expect his complete attention during their waking hours. They expect him to plan fun activities, to play with them, and to help them with their homework. He is their manservant. The children have responsibilities to nothing and no one but themselves. They are not asked to accommodate to the fact that their father has his own life and another primary relationship with his wife. At this point, they are satisfied customers, the father is a proud provider, and the wife feels left out. In therapy, I supported the wife's claims on loyalty from her husband and helped him see that his tunnel-vision dedication to his children was not good for them. He could be a better father by allowing more balance between his obligations to his wife and to his children.

Sometimes the original parent must defend the stepparent's rights when the children are interfering with those rights. In one family, the father's teenage daughters had always blasted the CD player until late at night, but their new stepmother went to bed at ten o'clock because she had to get up early. When she asked the girls to lower the music, they begrudgingly complied, then gradually dialed up the volume, only to repeat the same scenario the next night. I believed that the stepmother had a legitimate claim and deserved to be supported by her husband. Playing the CD player loud at night is not a fundamental right of childhood. Children sometimes confuse their preferences with their rights or needs. Stepfamily life requires a clear eye for that distinction.

Stepparents often feel out of control in their own households. Visible and non-ambivalent demonstrations of loyalty by the spouse, in areas where the children owe respect for the stepparent's needs, can improve the stepparent's morale and teach important lessons to the children. That is, children in stepfamilies have to learn to adjust to the needs of the new adult in the family, just as the new adult has to adjust to their needs.

For their parts, stepparents owe support and loyalty to the original parent, who often has the most complicated role in the family. Sometimes the stepparent becomes the in-house critic of the parent's child-rearing practices. Sometimes the stepparent gets jealous of the partner's attention to the children even when that attention is completely justified. Criticism and jealousy breed lack of confidence in original parents, who end up feeling they are not doing right in either roles as parent or spouse.

When children see themselves as voluntary consumers of family goods and services, they decline to become a real member of the new stepfamily. They refuse to become "naturalized" citizens of the new family. Sarah, a young adult who was raised in a stepfamily, taught me about this pattern. She said that for the first three years of her stepfamily, she deliberately kept her distance because her stepdad was trying to act like her real father. Although he was a good man and meant well, she wanted only one father in her life. It was only after the stepfather gave up and allowed her to have her distance that she came around. At about age sixteen, she said, "something went 'click.'" She decided to accept her mother's remarriage and to become a contributing member of the stepfamily.

All we can legitimately expect of our children in stepfamilies is that they show respect for their stepparent and their original parent, and that they fulfill the basic requirements of family citizenship: meals, chores, vacations, following the rules of the house. We can hope, but not demand, that they go farther to become contributors in the stepfamily and supporters of it. That degree of active involvement is something that children choose in their own heart and at their own time. But we should insist, for their good and our own, that they not go through stepfamily life as critical customers who are not getting the services they demand.

Do Away With the Term "Stepparent"

An irony about the loud music story I told before is that the children would probably have been more sensitive to the needs of an aunt if she had been living with them than they were with their stepmother. An aunt is not supposed to be a "mother," and therefore does not threaten a child's loyalty to the "real" mother. To a child, an aunt has always been around in the extended family, as opposed to the stepparent who entered later. And aunts can be close or distant without threatening the child's emotional equilibrium.

We know from the research on stepfamilies, such as in the work by James Bray, that it takes a number of years to be accepted as "parent-like" by children. A new stepparent who comes on too strong as a parental authority figure is one of the leading contributors to stepfamily failure. In other words, if the new stepparent acts too much like a parent, there is hell to pay with the children and in the marriage. On the other hand, if the stepparent does not invest enough in the children—does not act *enough* like a parent—there is still a price to pay. Finding the middle ground is very, very difficult.

The trajectories of adults and children are often out of sync in stepfamily life. Mom loves this guy deeply, sees him as good fathering material, and has never been happier. The kids are upset that their lives are turned upside down and that they must deal with a new quasi-father. She confidently expects the children will accept him and eventually come to treasure him as she does. He expects the same thing, since his love for her should carry over to her children. He wants to be a good father figure to them. Then reality hits when the children cast "no" votes in the election of this new stepparent.

Maybe it would be less confusing to everyone if we abandoned the odious term "stepparent" in favor of a new term that conveys the simple reality that "this is my parent's new spouse." Maybe we need a contest for a new name to describe the relationship between a child and a parent's spouse, a name that does not convey parenting authority and that does not immediately stir up loyalty conflicts for children. Here's a start: children could say, "this is my momsmate or my dadsmate"; adults could say, "this is my wifeskid or my husbandskid."

If you don't like these, try out some terms of your own. The idea is to create a new set of terms that will give some space and time for a new relationship to develop between the children and their parent's new spouse. Emotional overload and loyalty binds prevent many children from becoming active citizens of their stepfamilies. And once they have declined to sign up, their withdrawal takes on a life of its own. Using a word different from the loaded term "stepparent" could create the expectation that this new adult-child relationship will develop at its own pace. And someday, when the child says, "I feel like you are mother (or father) to me," that would be a moment of extreme joy—unexpected, not taken-for-granted joy.

Achieving Confident Parenting in Stepfamilies

Recently a good amount of research has been done about what it takes to make a stepfamily work for children and adults. The following ideas come from that research and my own learning from the families I have worked with or known personally:

- Work on your marriage. New remarriages can be fragile if not cultivated. Spend time alone with your spouse. Create rituals of connection such as going out on dates. Take marriage education courses to improve your communication skills. Make your marriage a high priority or the stresses of stepfamily life will erode it.

- Put yourself in your spouse's place. Try to grasp at a deeper level what it's like to be a stepparent or an original parent in a stepfamily. You have to get outside your own frustrations to see the experience of the other. For example, stepparents need to understand what it is like to feel pulled between the children and the spouse. Original parents need to understand what it's like to sometimes feel invisible and powerless in one's own home. You will have arrived at a deep mutual understanding when you can express your partner's true pain or frustration in your own words, so that your partner feels understood.

- Have empathy and understanding for the emotional world of the children. Often you have to listen between the lines, or read the children's behavior, because they are not able to express their deeper feelings directly. Understanding the pain of the children can especially help the stepparent not stay in a judgmental stance towards them. Children are usually not deliberately trying to make anyone's life miserable.

- Define your parental roles clearly. In nearly all cases, it is best for the original parent to be the lead parent, and for the stepparent to be a supporter or consultant. Allow time for the stepparent to develop an emotional bond with the children before expecting much in the way of disciplining.

- Clarify your expectations of what the children owe as citizens of the stepfamily. Not "liking" stepfamily life does not mean that the children become like borders in the house. Be clear about how you want them to contribute to the common good, and be firm in following up.

- Tolerate no disrespect for the stepparent (or for the original parent, for that matter). In stepfamilies, disrespect often comes in the form of ignoring the stepparent. In one family, the teenage girl would not say "hello" to her stepfather when he greeted her. That is disrespectful. The original parent must be vigilant in not tolerating this kind of behavior.

- Work on your family rituals. Starting a stepfamily gives you the chance to create new rituals and traditions, along with holding on to some old ones. Do not allow the children to opt out of family rituals such as dinnertime or family outings. You are sending them the message that family life is like a spectator sport: you can watch passively without participating.

- Allow for special rituals that do not involve all family members. It is especially important for original parents to have time alone with their children. Over time, it is helpful for the stepparent to create special time together with the children, such as going out for ice cream or to a ball game. But stepparents should be patient and let these rituals develop naturally.

- Join with other stepfamilies in support groups. No one knows what it's like better than other people in your situation. Don't try to do step family life alone.

A stepmother wrote me these words after a workshop dealing with stepfamilies: "I had no clue what I was getting into . . . I was in love! No one could have really prepared me for this, but I sure could have used a glimmer of some obstacles I would be running into." I thought of one of my favorite Far Side cartoons, which depicts a herd of lemmings running off a cliff into the sea. If a first marriage is a leap into unknown waters, most of us get the chance to adjust to the shallow waters before moving to the deep. But remarrying and creating an instant stepfamily is indeed a lemming-like experience. We are propelled by intense, mysterious desires to find a new life-mate, and so off the mountain we go into the sea, unprepared for its cold and depth. What attracts me most about the cartoon, however, is the depiction of one lemming, towards the back of the pack, with a smile on its face and an inner tube around its waist. When it comes to love—especially in the case of the second time around—we are all lemmings. Let's get busy distributing the inner tubes.

Unplugging Your Kids: Media and Child Rearing

We cannot raise responsible children unless we come to grips with what else is raising them. Bill Moyers, the public television commentator, once observed that our children are being raised by appliances. Television and the Internet are the electronic teachers of our children.

I confess that as a family therapist I used to pay little attention to the impact of media on children and families. It seemed too big and too pervasive to grapple with in working one-to-one with families. When my own children were young, I was generally aware of what they were watching on television, but did not pay close attention and did not set limits on the amount of time they spent watching TV. My twenty-three-year-old daughter recently commented that she is now surprised that we did not have more TV restrictions. Though I did have a clear sense that our children should not have television sets in their bedrooms, beyond that, I did not think much about the impact of television on their lives. Although my children have grown up well, I would pay more attention to television and all the media if I were raising children today.

I have become more concerned about television and the media in recent years, as I have read more about its negative effects on children, families, and communities. Most of the material presented in this chapter comes from David Walsh and his colleagues at the National Institute for Media and the Family, in Minneapolis.

My goal is to raise consciousness about a major problem in raising our children, so I will be strong and pointed in my comments about the media. But I also understand television's (and other media's) potential for good and I realize that simplistic prohibitions by parents restricting TV will not solve the problem. We have to learn to live with the media, minimize its negative impact, and heighten its potential positive impact on the raising of responsible citizens.

Television: The Sobering *Facts*

You are probably aware of the basic facts about the pervasiveness of television in the lives of our children, but perhaps you have not seen this information assembled in one place. Listed below is a summary of information about television and viewer habits garnered from a variety of reliable national surveys:

- The average child spends twenty-three hours per week watching television.

- Children spend more than twice as much time watching television as they do on schoolwork.

- The average number of television sets in a household with children is now 2.7, and is increasing steadily.

- Over half of American children have television in their bedroom. Not only do most adolescents watch television in their rooms, but now almost one-third of preschool age children have sets in their bedrooms.

- By age eighteen, children spend twice as much time watching television as they spend in a classroom.

- By age eighteen, children have seen 200,000 acts of violence on television, not counting the violence on video games. They have seen 20,000 murders.

- During the 7 to 8 p.m. time slot (once a defined family hour), eighty percent of television shows use four letter words, and sixty percent refer to sex.

- During all the prime time slots, seventy-four percent of all television shows contain sexual content.

- Despite this sexual saturation, television shows rarely make any reference to personal responsibility or personal risk. In one survey, only five percent of the shows with sexual content depicted any risks or responsibilities.

- Children are exposed to an estimated 10,000 food advertisements per year, mostly on television.

- Parents are not particularly concerned about the amount of television their children watch. In one survey, less than one-fourth of parents believe their child watches too much television.

- Parents are concerned, however, about the types of programs their children watch. One survey found that about sixy-two percent of parents say they provide "a great deal of supervision" over their children's television viewing. However, this percentage has been dropping, and about one-fourth of parents admit that their children watch inappropriate programs "sometimes" or "a great deal."

Television: The Sobering Effects

From a compendium of research, we know that exposure to television violence increases children's aggression toward their peers. We know that exposure to television commercials increases children's desires for consumer goods of all kinds. We know that the more television children watch, the less physically fit they are. We also know that the more television children watch, the lower their reading scores.

In addition to its effects on children as individuals, television affects the family as a whole. Television invades family rituals, especially dinner rituals, and it drains time away from possible family rituals such as playing cards or board games. Competition for the television is a big source of conflict between siblings in families. Control of the remote control often means having control of the family.

A program watched together by all family members at least provides opportunities for family discussion. But when children have television sets in their bedrooms, they are free to retreat into solitary space, without the possibility of conversation with their parents. Adolescents who have all of their electronic needs met in their bedrooms (television, CD player, computer, telephone) can tune out their families—except when they need parental services.

The effects go beyond the family. Television has been linked to the decline in participation in community activities. The most striking example was a town in the Arctic Circle where for generations the whole community gathered in one place on Thursday nights for socializing and discussing matters of common concern. Then television suddenly was introduced into the town's life. The Thursday night community ritual vanished almost immediately, as people stayed home in front of their television sets. It's not as if television was a novelty that wore off either: the community gathering never revived. Similar outcomes have occurred wherever in the world television was suddenly introduced into a community. Political scientist David Putnam believes that television is the principal culprit in the general decline in community participation in the past generation.

But let's face it: television watching is an enjoyable activity, or people wouldn't give up other experiences for it. In adults and children alike, television induces a trance-like state that, for a while, is pleasurable. Sometimes what we watch is funny, moving, entertaining, or educational. However, researchers have found that the pleasure goes down as the hours pile up. The people who report the most consistent pleasure in watching television are those who watch a specific show and then turn the set off. Watching passively from one show to the next, without the sense of making a choice, actually creates unpleasant feelings. But the trance-inducing quality of television makes it hard to turn it off, partly because at that point we don't know what else to do with ourselves.

What Television Teaches Our Children

Television is a diverse medium, and I don't want to indict all of it. Public television in particular strives to teach positive values. At its best, commercial television can inspire and educate. It can expose children to people from different ethnic groups. It can show how people live in different kinds of families. For example, *The Cosby Show* of the 1980s taught important lessons about family life in a funny, non-preaching style. My daughter and I used to watch *The Wonder Years* together every week, and would discuss how the episode spoke to coming of age. Television has great potential, and sometimes delivers on its potential. But by and large, television shows and commercials come with implicit values that make it harder to raise responsible children. Here are some of those negative values:

- Television nourishes a culture of disrespect.
  People are continually "dissing" one another on
  television. Disrespect is the source of most of
  the humor in comedies, and most of the
  tension in dramas.

- Television portrays parents as incompetent and befuddled, and children as wise (and smart alecky) beyond their years.

- Television teaches instant gratification, especially through commercials, where billions of dollars are spent to attract children (and adults) and to make them buy a product now.

- Television teaches that happiness is having things. The message that programming and commercials convey is that the good life is found in our purchases and our possessions.

- Television represents sex without commitment or consequences, either emotional or physical.

- Television desensitizes children to the effects of violence on human lives. It portrays aggression as no big deal.

Children and the Internet

Just as my parents' generation was the first to confront television in the lives of their children, today's parents must learn to deal with computers and the Internet. According to the Annenberg Center's recent survey on families and the media, computer and online technologies are the only media that are increasing their "penetration" in homes with children. Broadcast television, cable television, VCRs, video game equipment, and newspapers have all leveled off because most families already have them. But home computers increased by nearly fifty percent in at two-year period from 1996 to 1998. Internet or online services continue to increase, currently reaching over one-third of American households.

In the wake of several recent school massacres, a national debate began about the effects of computer video games on some of our youth. The two boys involved in the Littleton, Colorado killings had played hours of highly-violent video games. Experts say that a person can actually learn the hand-eye coordination needed to aim and shoot to kill through these video games. Other videos have disturbing combinations of sex and violence; for example, in one popular video game, the goal is to have sex with the enemy woman who is being pursued, and then kill her. For the most part, we parents are clueless about the content and tone of these videos.

As you might expect, middle and upper income families are more likely to have access to the Internet than poorer families, with nearly two-thirds of families with incomes over $75,000 having a subscription to an online service. Children with computers at home spend an average of forty minutes on line per day. Not all of these kids tune out the rest of the world. In fact, children with computers spend more time doing schoolwork and reading magazines or newspapers, although this is partly because they come from families with higher adult education and income.

The main challenge parents face with computers is children's access to all kinds of information—both positive and negative. From the World Wide Web, children can bring to their computer screen anything from educational materials to pornography to "chat rooms" whose participants are not monitored.

It is harder for parents to monitor children's use of the Internet than television. Television programs are listed and described in the newspaper, and there are a limited number of shows available at one time. The Internet has immense offerings available simultaneously. Material can be viewed on screen or downloaded for later viewing. And, for the most part, children are usually far more skilled than their parents in making their way around the World Wide Web.

The Internet is more diverse than television in terms of the values it teaches. At the positive end, it allows children to be active searchers for information and knowledge. It encourages communication, through e-mail, with friends and relatives. It encourages children to become computer literate. On the negative end, the Internet can teach that information is readily available without quality controls for its reliability.

And it can expose children to distorted images and messages about sexuality, the topic most frequently searched on the World Wide Web.

What Parents Can Do About the Media

If we are passive in the face of our children's electronic teachers—television and the Internet—they will have more influence than we do over our children's core values. For the most part, television teaches children to approach their lives as individualists, as pleasure seekers, as consumers—not as citizens with responsibilities to their families and communities. Even the Internet, with its outstanding opportunities for providing information, involves children mostly in a solo search for knowledge and fun. The Internet can connect children to others through e-mail and chat rooms, but recent research among college students indicates that too much electronic communication increases symptoms of depression. As humans, we are made to be social creatures. We are happiest when we are interacting productively and face-to-face with others.

Since these media are here to stay, what can we do as parents to emphasize their positive potential and offset their negative effects? The following are my suggestions, culled from experts in this area and from my own experience:

For Television
- Don't permit your children to have a television in their bedrooms. This encourages isolation from the rest of the family, and it is more difficult to monitor the programs they watch. If your child already has a television in his or her room, consider setting a window of time of a few months after which it will be removed. Be prepared for a major conflict, because your child will see this as a violation of a fundamental consumer right. That's why you need to give your child a good reason—to reduce isolation and provide better monitoring—and a family meeting to discuss it. If you are in a two-parent

family, do not remove a child's television without the unqualified support of your spouse, or the television will be back in the child's room before long.

- Decide in advance with your children which television shows they will watch each week. Make sure the television is off when one of those shows is not on. Do not let the television just stay on to provide background sight and sound.

- Utilize reviews and parent guides to learn about the content of current television programs.

- Watch television shows with your children to see what the shows are like and how your children are reacting to them. Discuss these shows with your children.

- Turn the television off during mealtimes.

- Do not use television programs as a babysitter to keep children occupied.

- Experiment with a TV-free night each week and use the gained time for family activities. Then experiment with a "TV-free" week each year.

- Set a good example in your own television watching by being deliberate about what you watch and don't watch.

For the Internet
- Have a rule that no chat rooms can be accessed without your previewing them for safety and age-appropriateness.

- Purchase a screening device to make sure that your young children cannot access sex sites on the Web.

- Limit the type and range of Web sites that your children can access.

- Do not permit your children to download anything from the Internet without coming to you for permission.

- Spend time searching the Web with your child. Teach your child how to distinguish between reliable and unreliable sources of information.

- Stay nearby and be attentive when your child is e-mailing and participating in chat rooms. You should do this not as a snoop, but as an interested and concerned parent.

- Violation of your Internet rules should bring immediate suspension of Internet privileges.

- Explain all of these policies to children during a family meeting. Tell them that your rules are not about your lack of trust for them, but about you doing your job of making sure they are safe.

For Video Games
- Carefully screen and monitor the video games your children bring home. Have a firm rule that no video game gets played until you have previewed it.

I do not want to make the media the scapegoat for why it is difficult to be a confident parenting raising responsible children. After all, we collectively created the media and now operate most facets. For the most part, television programs are produced by people who are themselves parents. The same is true for Web sites. We parents buy the products that are advertised. We parents are hooked on television as much as our children are. We ourselves are eager consumers. We permit media influence because the media reflect some of our collective values. The conflict is that most of us also have deeper values to pass on to our children. The problem is not just "out there" in the media, it is within each of us. There are community solutions to pursue, but in the meantime, there is no place like home for taking charge of how these appliances raise our children.

Resisting the Peer Cultures of Children and Parents

As we all know, the older children get, the more important their peer relationships become to them. Even though, as a parent of an adolescent, you retain a lot of influence on your child, your child's peers become like a constant houseguest—one that is demanding, unpredictable, and outside of your direct control besides. Imagine that this "houseguest" influences, more than you do, your teenager's attitudes towards sex and drugs, plus tastes in clothes, language, hair, looks, and music. This other child profoundly shapes your teenager's consumer desires and hence your household expenditures. If you declare war on this child, you risk driving your teenager into his or her arms. If you ignore this other child, you will surrender your own child to the peer culture.

It was not always so. Only in the last century have we created a peer culture of adolescence, with its own tastes and values. Previously, by the time most children reached puberty they were involved in the adult world as workers or apprentices. When we extended schooling until eighteen years old and beyond, and created laws against child labor, an entirely new phenomenon developed: the adolescent peer culture.

The teen peer culture really took off in the 1950s and 1960s. Take music as an example. When my father was growing up in the 1920s, the musical hits of the day were listened to by both teenagers and adults. So were the big radio programs. Once rock and roll entered the scene in the 1950s, teenagers had their own music and their own radio stations. Most teenagers became preoccupied with their status in a high-school peer group, whereas during prior generations the majority of teenagers were out of school and in the work force well before age eighteen. By the late 1960s, teenagers had adopted hairstyles and dress codes that were far different from those of the adult world. During the 1970s, teenagers increased their sexual activity far beyond their parents' comfort level, and they drastically increased their use of alcohol and drugs. Following Vietnam and Watergate, they embraced the growing American sentiment that government and adult authority were not to be trusted.

As economist Juliet Schor noted in her fascinating book, *The Overspent American*, it was the prosperous 1980s that brought on the consumer culture of youth. Corporations discovered that they could market successfully to the youth market. Casual shoes became the symbol of this exploding consumer youth culture. Brands such as Nike and Reebok pitched messages of status and prestige for kids who wore these expensive products. Designer jeans were not far behind. Madonna captured the spirit of the era as she intoned "We are living in a material world and I am a material girl." The mall replaced the soda shop and the street corner as youth hangouts.

Since the 1980s, the consumer culture of youth, fed by advertising and peer pressure, has moved alarmingly down the age ladder. Even four- and five-year-olds are aware of what is "in" and what is "out." They demand their Beanie Babies and their birthday parties at McDonald's. When you ask a seven-year-old what she wants for Christmas, you get a detailed list with brand names included. I know two grandparents who are amazed—and appalled—when they take their four-year-old granddaughter to the toy store. She marches down the aisles, thoroughly familiar with the merchandise, pointing to items and saying, "I want this" and "I want this one too, but I don't want that one." A discriminating shopper at age three!

You might argue that there is little harm in children having more choices as consumers. Isn't choice a good thing? The problem is that many of these purchases are driven, not so much by personal need or preference, but by a voracious peer culture fed by massive advertising programs. The push is to grow up quickly. Retailers report that girls as young as age six now insist on wearing teen designs. Many lines of classic girls' dresses are no longer available for this age group. Preteens now want to wear the revealing fashions of teenagers, including brands with names such as "Streetwalkers."

It's not that most parents want their children to dress beyond their years, but that they cannot resist their children's advertising-driven demands. The Wall Street Journal recently reported "a fundamental shift in children's buying patterns over the past several years. Moms and dads may still pay for their children's clothing, but kids are picking out the clothes themselves." In another newspaper article, a Target executive described witnessing the fierce but losing battles that mothers are fighting with their daughters in the stores. I was stunned to read that just one of Target's brands, according to this executive, is "designed for seven- and eight-year-olds whose mothers are still impacting the purchase decision." Retailers know a trend when they see one. Without adult protection, the consumer culture shortens the time that our children can be children.

There are other peer social pressures not directly related to consumerism. Many twelve-year-olds have steady boyfriends or girlfriends. Coed sleepovers begin at this age. Girls start dieting. Boys strive for the cool, disheveled look. Popularity with both sexes is the goal of early adolescent life. You no doubt recognize these pressures from your own adolescence, but most observers believe they are more intense now, involve more visible consumer goods, and begin at earlier ages. In a world lacking confident adult authority figures at home and in school, the peer culture of adolescence is more potent than ever.

Parental Peer Pressure

Lest we think of peer pressure as an alien invasion, keep in mind that we adults are not immune to pressure from our own peers. Children absorb their values from their families, from the media, and from the larger community. If children are taken with the consumer culture, it's because we are too. If twelve-year-olds have coed sleepovers, it's because somebody's parent thinks it's cute and permits it. If fifteen-year-olds have beer kegs at parties, it's because an adult purchased it for them. It's the parents who rent the hotel room for the night of the senior prom. If youth are more distrustful of adult authority, they learned it from their baby boomer parents. Kids learned to give in to peer pressure from their parents.

Parental peer pressure is one of the dirty little secrets of contemporary family life. Keeping up with other parents is behind much of our difficulty in handling our children's peer-driven demands. When every other child in the school has an expensive birthday party, we want nothing less for our own son or daughter. We justify it as something nice for our child, but in truth we don't want to be out of step with our peers. We don't want to come up short as parental service providers.

Parental peer pressure starts early, and children notice it from a young age. We want our three-year-old to wear designer overalls, even if the generic brand is just as good and fits our budget. Even parents who say they resist the consumer culture brag that they bought the designer clothes at a big discount. We want our child to be in the best preschool in order to have a leg up academically by kindergarten. We are afraid that if we do not start our child in piano and soccer by age six, they will have missed a key opportunity—and it will be our fault. We want so much for our eleven-year-olds to fit in, and to excel at something, that we push them towards the traveling soccer team with its heavy expenses in money and family time. We over-schedule our children in order not to be seen as holding them back. Who brags about a kid having time to hang around and entertain himself?

When our children become teenagers, competitive parenting makes us not want to deny them anything that their peers trumpet. What is wrong, we ask ourselves, with a television in their bedroom, with a private telephone line, with a closet full of expensive clothes? Having grown up entitled to goods and services from parents, our teenagers are expert advocates for their consumer rights. And once they get their own paid jobs, our control over their purchases nearly vanishes. If you are too miserly to do your duty as a parent, they suggest, then they will pay for the extra telephone line or the television or the expensive sneakers. Unless the purchase or activity is clearly dangerous or illegal, how do you say "no" to an American teenager who has the money to make it happen?

But once again, it's not just the kids. As Juliet Schor has documented, we adults, especially since the 1980s, have become more preoccupied with keeping up with what we think is the American standard of living. We adopt new technologies, such as cell phones and fax machines, with unprecedented speed. We upgrade our computers when the old ones work fine. We upscale our transportation by purchasing expensive sports utility vehicles that are not really any better for most of us than a regular automobile. We bring a latte to work rather than drink the regular coffee supplied there. Our new houses are getting larger as our average family size is shrinking. Our 1950s kitchen becomes unacceptable and must be remodeled. The status and expense of a product or service comes to signify its quality or usefulness. Our wants become our needs in an escalating pattern of acquisition. And our children notice all this and learn.

Lest I sound like the critic of everyone else, let me tell you that I feel the same consumer pressures. I drink lattes. I upgrade my computer every couple of years. I am considering getting a home fax machine. The last two automobiles we bought were new ones, even though I know that the economics of car ownership clearly points to buying a late model used car and saving on the depreciation. But I wanted a new car, and we had the money. Now it will be hard to not buy a new car when the old one gives out. I tell myself that I have drawn the line in other important areas. Our children went to good public schools, not private schools. We live in a nice house but we could afford a more expensive one. We drive our cars for ten years or more, instead of four or five. But the full truth is that I, like everyone else, must continually balance my life between wants and needs.

The sad irony of the adult consumer culture is that most of us are earning more money and spending more money, but are feeling less materially satisfied. According to Juliet Schor's research, nearly forty percent of people earning between $50,000 and $100,000 feel that they cannot afford to buy everything they really need. Believe it or not, twenty-seven percent of those with incomes over $100,000 feel the same way. The best explanation for this phenomenon is that we are continually upgrading our expectations for what we should possess, based on our sense of what the people whom we identify with have. We therefore spend more of our income, and save less, than any other industrialized country in the world. The problem, I have come to believe, is not that we purchase or possess too much, but that we do so for the wrong reasons. We have become competitive consumers.

In this world of escalating ambitions, parenting becomes a competitive sport. We want our child to be the best, or at least to have the best opportunities. We fear that they will lose ground to the competition—other kids who are better served by their own parents. One mother was crestfallen when her daughter did not get accepted to an elite New York City preschool. The reason for the rejection was like a dagger in the mother's heart: her daughter was "not mature enough." We're talking about a three-year-old here! Some parents are already planning for their preschooler's eventual entrance into an elite college, which is why an elite preschool is so important to them.

I talked to a woman who moved her family out of a wealthy Minneapolis suburb after attending the first grade orientation. There she encountered a number of parents who were openly weighing whether to hold back their sons from first grade for another year. Not because the children were developmentally behind, but in order to make them a year older than their peers when they played varsity hockey ten years hence. Here parenting as a competitive sport is no metaphor; it's the real thing. The mother I talked to realized that she could not raise her children in that type of an atmosphere and had to move.

What We Can Do

It should be clear where I think we have to start to correct the problem of parental peer pressure: with ourselves. Most of us are as blind as our teenagers at seeing how peer pressure influences our decisions. Although we notice when many other parents around us are into competitive, materialistic parenting, it's hard to recognize it within ourselves. But we are all influenced by the consumer and peer cultures. It's in the air we breathe, the water we drink. If we do not face its role in our families, then we cannot figure out how to make changes.

Once we confront the culture of competitive parenting in ourselves, we will be able to deal more constructively with peer influences on our children. Our kids sense our insecurities. But they also sense when we are regaining confidence in finding our own path. They take their cues from us.

Here are some ideas about coming to grips with parental peer pressure:

- Increase your awareness of consumerism and the competitive culture of parenting as you see them around you.

- Do the soul searching needed to see how these forces influence your own decisions as a consumer. I am not urging you to collapse into guilty self-reproach, but do not let yourself off the hook either. For each major consumer decision, try assigning a percentage to estimate the influence of peer expectations. A certain amount of parental peer influence is inevitable and probably good. But is this influence driving your decision?

- Before making decisions about parenting, pause to ask yourself about the motivations and pressure involved. Go deeper than simply saying "my child needs or wants this" or "we can afford it." For example, you can ask yourself if you had this item or this activity when you were a child, and whether not having it handicapped you. Weigh the difference between your child feeling completely out of it with a peer group, versus your child being a consumer leader of the peer group.

- Pay close attention to all the costs (not just the money costs) involved in purchasing goods or services for your child: the time costs, the unavailability of those funds for something else, the extra hours of work you may have to do, the loss of family time, the erosion of family rituals, the loss of unstructured time.

- Try to determine what is "good enough" for your children as opposed to what is "optimal." You may want to pursue what is optimal in one area, say, music, if your child is musically talented. But striving for optimal opportunities in multiple areas will put you and your child on a permanent treadmill. Your piano player does not necessarily have to be on the traveling soccer team or get a black belt in karate by age twelve.

- Talk with your co-parent about all of this. If one of you is weak in this area you both will succumb to competitive parenting.

- Talk with other parents in your school, neighborhood, or religious community. There is strength in numbers of resisters. We need a mass movement to counteract the power of the consumer culture of childhood and parenthood.

Here are some ideas for parents to deal with the peer influences on your children:

- Know your children's friends—their names, their tastes, their personalities.

- Know these friends' parents. Organize periodic gatherings among the parents of your children's friends, as my colleague Jim Levine did.

- Listen to what the peers are saying when you are carpooling. Kids have a way of forgetting a parent is with them in the car.

- Insist that certain family times and family rituals take priority over time with peers.

- Hold firm to your rules about dating, curfews, and drinking. Talk with the other parents about their rules and expectations, so that your teenager does not paint you as the only parent with these standards.

- Involve your child and your family in a religious community, especially one that gets youth involved in community work.

- Tell your children what you like about their friends. Being positive allows you to deliver cautions at times without your child feeling you're always negative about all his or her friends.

- When you have a specific concern about a friend of your child, couch your criticism as concern for what problems the child may be dealing with. For example: "When I hear Jeff joke about getting drunk, I worry about him." Avoid directly attacking the friend's personality.

- Involve your child in a volunteer, community building activity with the rest of the family.

- When it comes to buying brand-name consumer items for your child, find a balanced approach you are comfortable with. With our children, my wife and I occasionally bought them designer items, as a partial concession to the junior high peer culture, but mostly we did not.

- At peaceful moments, share your own values about the challenges that teenagers face, such as sex, drugs, and peer pressure. The evidence is quite clear that these conversation are very influential.

- Do not surrender to the busyness of the teen peer culture. Hold onto your child and your family.

It takes considerable courage to raise responsible children in a culture that encourages self-interested consumption of what the world offers, and in a culture where so many of us are preoccupied with not losing ground to our peers. Ultimately, our success at the venture of growing good citizens depends on our own citizenship—and our courage to expect a great deal of ourselves and our children.

William J. Doherty is a professor of family social science and director of the Marriage and Family Therapy Program at the University of Minnesota. He continues his practice as a marriage and family therapist—as he has done for the past 22 years. A sought-after public speaker, Doherty offers lectures and workshops across the country on family-life issues, presenting a message that "cuts across ideological lines." His most recent book, *The Intentional Family*, shows how families can use everyday rituals to improve the quality of their relationships. The parents of two grown children, Doherty and his wife, Leah, live in Roseville, MN.